What the World Needs Now ...

90 Days to a Happier Life

For our sisterhood!
Love,
Carol

By

Carol Barbour

For Daddy and Uncle Harold,

two of the most spiritually gifted men

I've ever known …

INTRODUCTION

The past fifteen years are the most tumultuous I've experienced. My ex-husband divorced me to marry his pregnant girlfriend. I lost my job as an elementary school principal when school system administrators abruptly added my school to the closure list in hasty, questionable circumstances. I accepted an appointment in another district and that became a turbulent experience when a group of "elite" parents and faculty members opposed instructional and staffing changes I made. In response, they organized an email campaign and provided a news reporter with half-truths to advance their agenda. In the midst of their covert actions, my father was diagnosed with cancer and news cameras filmed an opinion story about what a horrible principal and person I was, all during the same week. The reporter never interviewed me and I never had an opportunity to defend myself. After two consecutive difficult experiences, I resigned the position and returned home to spend more time with my family, help care for and support my father during his radiation treatments and to look for another job.

Despite successful community interviews and final interviews with several superintendents, I wasn't hired. Several years later, I discovered I wasn't selected because of a poor reference from my last superintendent and the sensationalistic news story. I was mystified. The superintendent never observed me, visited the school or told me there was a problem with my performance. The half truths the reporter shared in the broadcast, swollen with "shock factor" and abject bias, are on the internet for the world to see. Despite a reference letter that made the circumstances clear, school systems assumed the poor reference and news story were accurate without giving me an opportunity to share my truth.

After interviewing for thousands of positions over the past six years, I still haven't been hired. During the first year and a half of my search, I became embittered and angry, sinking into a pit of self-pity. I complained and whined, wallowed in frustration, stonewalling my own progress. My father, a very forthright man who loved me with his entire heart, said he was tired of listening to me complain about my circumstances and dwelling in negativity. He told me to speak life, exercise my faith and use my God given gifts to move forward. My eyes watered. My face burned. My hands shaking, I ended our conversation.

Daddy stunned me when he spoke to me that way. He always comforted me when I was in pain, encouraging me that everything would be alright. I was angry because I thought he was ignoring how unkindly and unfairly I had been treated. I reflected on our conversation throughout that day and realized he was right. He didn't negate my feelings. He wanted me to realize how much worse things would become if my attitude didn't change. He wanted me to leave my self-imposed prison of self-pity and shattered hope. Ultimately, Daddy wanted me to *get out of my own way*. This pivotal conversation led to my most critical epiphany. That evening, I thanked my father for his honesty.

From that evening forward, I chose life and light again. I remembered that each day it is up to me to choose happiness, positivity and love. Things didn't change overnight. I became more resilient and faithful while facing foreclosure, a heart disease and the challenge to become healthier without medical insurance. Choosing positivity and happiness brought an immense peace and freedom once I decided to embrace every opportunity with hope and joy. That conversation changed my life and put me back on a positive course. I created an inspirational Facebook page called Carol's Notes and shared original Notes of encouragement and inspiration for others based on what I'd learned through my own despair and disappointments.

Three years after this crucial conversation, my father died suddenly from a post-surgical blood clot. His words three years earlier resonated, helping me cope with the enormity of losing him forever. Even in grief I remained determined to move forward and refused to give up on living a happy life while serving God, helping others and honoring my father's legacy.

Life will always change us, challenge us and mold us. It's our responsibility to remember that we have the power through God, our faith in Him and every Gift of The Spirit to face and defeat our challenges one by one. It's not, however, an easy thing to do for ourselves, let alone to help others to do. It's easy to tell people what they should do but we don't often enough stay the course with them to love and support them through the process. That's why I wrote this book. I've shared daily reflections to show you how to love others and yourself, how to hold on to your hope and joy and how important it is to have faith, pray, meditate and to speak life into every situation.

Your life won't radically change simply because you've read this book but I guarantee developing and using the Gifts of The Spirit in your life will lead you to a happier, more fulfilling life. The nine Gifts are love, joy, peace, patience, kindness, goodness, faithfulness, humility and self-control, exactly what our world needs more of from each of us. I hope this book guides you toward an even happier, more peaceful and fulfilling life with happier relationships and that you become a blessing to others.

Day 1: Love

What our world needs more of than anything else is unconditional love and compassion for others. There are several ways we can increase love and compassion without spending a dime and we can do it in seconds with minimal effort. First, we can love and accept ourselves as we are. We must make room for self-love and self-acceptance in order to grow and love others. Self-love and self-acceptance pave the way for us to love and accept others as they are. Acceptance is the first step toward friendship among people. So many people are unhappy because others judge them. What amazing friendships we would have if we accepted one another as we are instead of trying to make people conform to what we want them to be.

	It's easier to accept one another when we relate to our commonalities rather than focusing on our differences. We all feel the exhilaration of love and emotions of despair when someone we love dies. We know what rejection feels like. It's painful, often tortuous. Thinking more about our commonalities redirects our focus more to what brings us together instead of what pulls us apart. When we love and accept ourselves, we're able to think more about what unites us with others. We become more adept at bringing out the best in others because we see them with eyes of acceptance and hearts of love. We see the best in others when we look for it.

Children are the best examples of unconditional love. They play together and enjoy one another's company without respect to race, ethnicity, finances and so many other complications adults introduce to their relationships. They're honest with one another when mistakes are made. Children talk about what happened and quickly move on. Wouldn't it be wonderful if we followed their example?

We CAN … if we choose to.

Today's Affirmation:

I will remember I'm worthy of self-love. I'm uniquely gifted and I know others are gifted and also worthy of love and acceptance.

DAY 2: JOY

People don't steal our joy, we surrender it to them. Each of us is the commander in chief of our joy and we must never allow anyone else to control it. If anyone had an excuse to dwell on her misery and drown in self-pity, Anne Frank did while she and her family were forced to hide, living secretly in a cramped attic with another family to escape Nazi occupation and persecution. Anne chose to write in her diary, holding onto the joy and hope of becoming a writer once the war was over. After the Nazis stormed their hiding place, the next glimpse of the world Anne saw was a miserable life in several concentration camps. Anne and her sister Margot, ripped away from their parents, died alone as prisoners in their final concentration camp. I can't imagine how difficult it must have been to be a young girl so curious about the world and having to learn about it through books because of a ghoulish hatred she and her family couldn't escape. In the worst of circumstances, this young girl refused to surrender her joy and hope for a better life and because of her strength, we learned about her family's story through Anne's diary.

Before Oprah Winfrey became the mogul and icon she is today, she lost her job as a news anchor when producers decided she wasn't "appealing enough" for television. What if Oprah had wallowed in the pain of rejection rather than holding onto hope and joy and pursuing her dream? Oprah chose to hold on to the positivity in her life and reused to give up. She worked diligently and achieved more than those producers who rejected her could possibly have imagined. Instead of appearing on a network, Oprah *owns* a network.

It's easy to dwell on our misery and problems but it's a very harmful outlook. When we dwell on our challenges, we leave little energy to exercise our faith and happiness. Just as our words our powerful, so are our thoughts. No matter what happens, there is always something beautiful to appreciate and a joy that can't be contained. Focus on the beauty that remains. Believe in your future. Become a prisoner of hope and watch your joy increase!

Today's Affirmation:

I will focus on a joyful future. Nothing in my past has any bearing on my future.

DAY 3: PEACE

One of the toughest decisions we often have to make is whether we should hold on to someone or something we love or let go. These are the times we have to hold onto our inner peace rather than following a person or plan that disturbs our peace. In fact, the people and things we fight to hold onto most passionately are sometimes the obstacles holding us back.

I remember dating a man I cared for very deeply. Despite the love I felt for him, he was not a good potential mate. Our core values clashed. The things he didn't appreciate about me, such as my spirit of encouragement and kindness, are things I value because I believe they are my spiritual gifts. I exhausted too much energy holding onto a dead situation. Once I released this misdirected energy, I met a wonderful man who cares about me exactly as I am, a very wonderful thing indeed. Sometimes, no matter how much we love someone, no matter how badly we believe we want something, it's just not right for us and we do more harm to ourselves by fighting for what we should release and we lose ourselves and our peace in the process.

What's meant for us won't require a struggle. It won't disturb our inner peace. We won't have to face a battle at every turn. Sometimes the battle between hanging on and letting go is a matter of ego, pride, loneliness or desperation, when what we must hold onto most firmly is our inner peace and inner strength. Make it a point to do what's best for you. Hold onto to your peace instead of fighting to prove your pride or ego. Don't wrestle with things that rob you of peace of mind. One of the best life lessons is recognizing when a win isn't worth the battle and frustration. There are some battles we shouldn't fight even if we can win. There are other battles we should fight that we won't win. Knowing when to let go is a win that adds to our peace.

Today's Affirmation:

I will remain at peace. I won't force any outcomes in my life and draw myself out of my peace.

DAY 4: PATIENCE

I grew up hearing my mother say Patience is a virtue. Patience is a very positive trait, one we should show to others, yet we often fail to be as patient as we should be with ourselves. Life would be much happier and easier if we showed ourselves more patience and kindness. One of the prime reasons it is essential to be patient with ourselves is because of our personal growth. In order to grow and become stronger, we have to love ourselves enough to be patient as we strive toward our goals. Think of it this way. Babies stumble and fall continuously but they don't become angry with themselves. They don't decide to crawl forever. They continue trying until they're able to walk. That's patience in action!

Just as we must love ourselves before we can love others, we have to know how to be patient with ourselves to accept others. When we're impatient with ourselves, we can drown in depression and unhappiness. Depression and unhappiness cause us to withdraw from life. We become bitter and unable to cope. Becoming patient with ourselves helps us to conquer the difficulties we face, both large and small, with courage rather than frustration and directly rather than through avoidance.

We become incredibly powerful through patience. Self-patience is one of our most powerful life coping skills. Though it seems counterintuitive, patience is a form of compassion and a way to free ourselves from the consequences of negative emotions. Being patience with ourselves is incredibly liberating and it empowers us to invest in others, to react more in love than frustration and disapproval. It prevents us from becoming perfectionists. We learn to celebrate smaller victories and encourage ourselves along the way to the bigger victories.

Being patient is a choice. Today, choose to be patient, especially with yourself. Even if you have to take baby steps until you master the art of self-patience, don't give up!

Today's Affirmation:

I will be patient with myself. My patience with self helps me to be patient with others.

DAY 5: KINDNESS

One of my favorite biblical stories since childhood is The Good Samaritan. A Jewish man is traveling from Jerusalem to Jericho on a road with several nooks and places where a robber or band of robbers could hide and ambush a traveler. He's robbed, beaten and left for dead. After this man's near death experience, we meet several other characters. Several passersby saw the injured man before The Good Samaritan came along, including a priest and a Levite.

The priest crossed the street to avoid the injured man without looking back. He was a leader in the synagogue, yet he didn't stop to help another in need. He was cold and purposely avoided someone in need. The second person, a Levite, didn't show compassion either. Levites served religious and political duties among Israelites, yet the Levite didn't think it was important to help a stranger. The third passerby, The Good Samaritan, was considered by the Jews as beneath them because they were non-believers. The Good Samaritan not only stopped to tend to the man's injuries but he also took him to an inn and paid for his lodging and continued care, promising to reimburse any additional expenses incurred during the man's recovery. The Good Samaritan went above and beyond what is expected to show kindness and compassion to a stranger.

Thank goodness for people like The Good Samaritan who uplift us when the rest of the world beats us down. He was a shining example in a sometimes cold and uncaring world. Everyone deserves love and compassion no matter what their race, religion, sexual orientation or any other characteristics are. It's easy to help our friends and family but it's also important to help those we don't know. We should help people whether they can return our kindness and time or not. Let this be the day you help someone in need without hesitation and without expecting anything in return.

Today's Affirmation:

I will be compassionate and loving. I care about how other people feel and I have a heart for others.

DAY 6: GOODNESS

People who focus on helping others are true heroes to me. Those who overcome their struggles and have hearts that brim with goodness and compassion are giants. No matter what happens in our lives, we cannot allow it to prevent us from having a spirit of goodness.

I learned a few things about Keanu Reeves recently that make me consider him a giant of goodness and compassion. Keanu has faced and overcome adversity that would make most people embittered with self-pity, pessimism and ready to give up. His father abandoned him when he was just three years old. As a dyslexic student, a disorder that's difficult to deal with, Keanu attended four high schools. Discouraged, he dropped out of high school.

When he was 23 years old, his best friend died from a drug overdose. He met a woman with whom he fell in love. A year later their daughter was stillborn. The pain of this tragedy tore their relationship apart. Not even two years later, his estranged wife died in a car accident. One of Keanu's greatest triumphs came when his younger sister survived leukemia. He gave seventy percent of his profits from his starring role in *The Matrix* to medical facilities that treat leukemia. Helping to improve the lives of other people on a grand scale is an amazing, faith filled response to tragedy and unhappiness. This is goodness in action.

Keanu is quoted on social media saying, "I think we can all pretty well agree that even n the face of tragedy, a stellar person can thrive. No matter what's going on in your life, you can overcome it. Life is worth living." It is a beautiful and wonderful thing for a person who has experienced personal tragedies to continue to love others and have an attitude of goodness and love. Any gift or act of love from the heart is an example of goodness. Be encouraged from this moment forward to be a stellar person who thinks of others and who focuses on the goodness of life and chooses not to merely survive but to thrive with a spirit of goodness.

Today's Affirmation:

I will help others and be a giant of goodness in my community.

DAY 7: FAITHFULNESS

True friends are rare jewels. One of the most treasured traits a friend can have is faithfulness. We want our friends to be loyal, trustworthy and consistent, normal and completely acceptable expectations. Loyalty is a true, constant support from another person. Loyal friends are always there to support us with unending love. Loyalty means our friends correct us in love rather than discussing our shortcomings with other people. In a world like ours that is driven by social media and whims, having a loyal friend is more valuable than striking oil.

Along with loyalty, another important aspect of faithfulness among friends is trustworthiness. Our friends should be people we can rely on, people who will hold our confidences and speak well of us when we're not around. The friendship vault of confidences should always be locked and guarded. Genuine friends uphold us rather than betraying us to idle gossip.

Loyalty and trustworthiness are both gifts and made more precious with consistency. Truly consistent friends are present during our happy and challenging times. They are an interwoven presence in our memories. It's easy to be a fair-weather friend who's around during the best of times but being a pillar of strength during sad and challenging times is true faithfulness among friends.

When I think of loyal friends, David and Jonathan come to mind. They were loyal to one another during lean and rich times. When David married Jonathan's sister, they became brothers. Jonathan's love for David didn't change when David replaced Saul as Israel's king. Even after Jonathan died, David continued to be loyal to his friend by caring and providing for Jonathan's son Mephibosheth. Let their friendship built on love encourage you to be the best friend you can be.

Today's Affirmation:

I will be a faithful friend who is true, constant and loyal.

DAY 8: HUMILITY

Each of us has experienced moments when we've been hurt by another person's words or actions when we didn't deserve it. Insults and hurtful deeds cause pain and make us want to lash out when we have every right to be angry and feel hurt. I worked for an organization where a portion of employees who reported to me said unkind, untrue things about me amongst each other and in the community, to management and to the media. Adding insult to injury, the media outlet did not attempt to verify any of their statements with me before they aired the story.

Their wholesale of untruths and exaggerations damaged the trajectory of my career and created other challenges for me as well. I had every right to sue the individuals who slandered me, the organization for which I worked and the media outlet that so irresponsibly reported the story. After talking with my father, I decided to be gentle, or humble, and show them the grace and mercy they failed to show me.

Sometimes we have to show people the mercy we didn't receive from them. As difficult as it is to do, showing mercy to those who don't deserve it builds character and it's always an appropriate response. The things that don't break us make us stronger. We have to choose to rise to the occasion. I often think of The Prodigal Son's father when I think of humility and grace in action. This father did not have to accept his son with open arms when he returned home after having the audacity to claim his inheritance and going out into the world and squandering his father's hard work. Yet, he did, showing an exceptional forgiveness and love.

The high road isn't always easy to travel but there are rarely traffic jams. We also won't have to take unnecessary detours. Let's decide today to be gentler to others and to the world than others and the world have been to us.

Today's Affirmation:

I will show others the mercy and love I want to receive when I'm wrong. I can make the world a less cold and unloving place with humility.

DAY 9: SELF-CONTROL

The human mind and body are the most brilliant creations in our world's history. Each of us has a unique, unduplicated fingerprint. Our bodies can adapt to virtually any climate and terrain. We can train our bodies with weight lifting to become stronger and leaner. As amazing as our bodies are, they're pale in comparison to the power and wonder of our minds.

We have the ability to laugh and recognize humorous situations. One of life's simple pleasures is laughing and sharing jokes with friends. We can admire and treasure the beauty around us. A dear friend recently visited the Grand Canyon and the photos she shared are breathtakingly beautiful. We can also experience love for one another. Of every memory, one of the most fluid we experience is our first love.

The power of wisdom is the most astounding ability we have because we can choose our thoughts. It takes discipline and dedication to set our minds but it can be done. It's essential for us to harness the power of our minds because what we ponder and the thoughts we dwell on influence our attitudes, behavior and the outcomes of our futures. We can use self-control and it is up to us to decide what kinds of thoughts to entertain. If we dwell on depressing topics, we will feel depressed. When we dwell on happy thoughts and memories, we set a pleasant tone for ourselves.

My Aunt Elaine was one of the most positive people I've ever known. She didn't have a bad word to say about anyone and if someone did something wrong, she would always say they must have had a reason and to look for the good in them. It took an enormous amount of self-control for her to set her mind to think this way. Set yourself up for monumental success by dwelling on the positives with powerful thoughts. Focus on all of the good things that can and will happen. Choose positive, fruitful and peaceful thoughts. You have the power so harness it!

Today's Affirmation:

I will use self-control and focus my thoughts. I choose to be positive and peaceful.

DAY 10: LOVE

Everyone wants and deserves love and we want to love others too. Sometimes we're so hurt from our disappointments or anger at someone we love, we feel weary and discouraged. It's a vicious cycle because hurt people hurt people. Truth be told, it's up to each of us to stop the cycle of anger, hurt and disappointment.

Anger is disappointed love. It isn't always easy to forgive people when they hurt us but it's a vital step to take. We have to remember that sometimes when people hurt us, it isn't about us. How many times has someone lashed out an another for an offense they didn't commit? How often do we take our anger out on the wrong person?

Someone has to break the cycle of hurt and disappointment. We can't wait for everyone else to step up so it's a responsibility we must all share. They only antipode we have for anger, hurt and disappointment is love and love is our best weapon. One way we can show love and break the cycle is by giving forgiveness when we are wrong. When conflicts go unresolved, there is no room for healing but when we value one another enough to break the cycle by digging deeply enough to resolve our differences, we begin the healing process.

The main reason we need to forgive is for our own sakes. Our internal pain, disappointments and anger don't do us or the people we love any favors. When we resent , are disappointed in ourselves and angry about our mistakes, we cut ourselves off from the world and shrink back from all we have to offer. Self-forgiveness is a form of love and it includes reconciling our mistakes and moving forward, lessons learned.

Love yourself today enough to forgive yourself for any past mistakes. Love those around you by forgiving them if they've hurt or disappointed you. Do your part to break the cycle of anger, hurt and disappointment.

Today's Affirmation:

I will break the cycle of hurt in my life and help those I love to break their cycles of hurt.

DAY 11: JOY

Joy is a beautiful feeling, a euphoria we want to hold onto with every fiber of our strength. The beautiful thing about the kind of joy we feel deeply in our hearts is that it's so pure and from our souls. Joy comes from hearing a child's laughter. We can feel immense joy when we recall a special memory. Nostalgic joy comes when we hear an old song that reminds us of an old love or our school days. We also get a great deal of joy when we do things from our souls for others without expecting anything in return.

It's our responsibility to maintain our inner joy. No one gave it to us and no one can take it away. It isn't easy to remain joyful because we will face difficult times. As a musician, I know the background stories behind many hymns. The song "It Is Well With My Soul," written by Horatio Spafford, is all about holding onto your joy and peace despite our circumstances. A wealthy attorney, he suffered a series of losses that would be difficult for anyone to handle. His son died and the majority of his investments burned in the Great Chicago Fire. He realized his family needed a vacation so he sent his wife and daughters on a voyage ahead of him to Europe. Tragically, all of his remaining children drowned in a shipping accident. His wife was the only survivor. He boarded another ship to meet his wife and during that voyage, he penned the touching lyrics, When sorrows like sea billows roll, it is well with my soul.

It takes a strong person to maintain a grateful and joyful mindset in the midst of the calamity Spafford and his family faced. As challenging as it is to remain joyful in difficult circumstances, we have to be grateful for the joy we have even in our most difficult times because sometimes that is all we have to push ourselves forward.

Today's Affirmation:

I will hold onto my joy. I appreciate every moment of happiness in my life and I will savor it, even in my toughest times.

DAY 12: PEACE

Being at peace is an inside job. This is one of the simplest, most helpful truths we can embrace. No matter what we experience from external sources, we can still be at peace if we choose to. Each of us is the CEO of our own lives. A person who was familiar with this truth is Corrie ten Boom. I learned so much about her while reading her book *The Hiding Place*.

Corrie ten Boom, a Dutch Christian, aided countless Jews in escaping the Holocaust. She and her family risked everything to help others when they needed it most. After an informant reported their family for helping Jews, they were imprisoned. Once they were imprisoned, Corrie and her sister Betsie were transferred from prison to several concentration camps. Despite being imprisoned in a concentration camp, Corrie and Betsie continued worshipping and believing through a Bible they snuck into prison with them. Betsie died, leaving Corrie alone at the camp until World War II ended.

The concentration camp didn't stop Corrie. Once she was free, she returned home to The Netherlands and served others again by helping Holocaust survivors become gainfully employed. She even helped some of the people who betrayed her family. Corrie's work earned worldwide acclaim and many honors. She wrote multiple books, sharing her story with the world. If a woman like Corrie could be imprisoned, tortured and abused in a concentration camp and hold on to her inner peace and faith while continuing to serve others for the rest of her life, imagine what we can do too.

No one is at peace because of their circumstances. Peaceful people are able to be calm and content in every situation because of their mindset and attitude. Hold onto and protect your peace and help others when you can.

Today's Affirmation:

I will be at peace even in difficult, trying times. I am responsible for holding onto my peace in every situation.

DAY 13: PATIENCE

Our happiest times are wonderful to experience. Who doesn't want to celebrate the good things, the joyous moments and victories? Yet, as wonderful as our best moments are, we develop the best of our traits and greatest strengths during times of adversity. Helen Keller, an amazing woman who was the first deaf and blind person to earn a college degree, knew exactly what it meant to face and overcome adversity.

Helen developed a serious illness as a toddler that caused her to lose her abilities to hear and see. She became very difficult to handle, often having long fits of screaming. Helen also broke household items and often bit or kicked family members. Despite their circumstances, Helen's parents remained patient, refusing to give up on her, even when family members and friends suggested Helen should be committed. Helen's life and the life of her family turned around once she became Anne Sullivan's student. Anne, herself visually impaired, taught Helen to communicate by touch and Braille.

Helen became a humanitarian, an educator and a writer in a situation where so many would have given up and when many would have given pity rather than expecting Helen to succeed against the odds. Her life and accomplishments became the plot of the Broadway Play The Miracle Worker, which also became a feature film.

You will face adversities you don't want to endure and overcome struggles you never thought you'd survive. Be patient because some challenges won't be conquered overnight. Pull from the strength of what you've overcome and know there's always a positive purpose for every negative experience. Every negative that comes your way is an opportunity to become stronger and more patient.

Today's Affirmation:

I will be patient while facing obstacles. My faith reassures me I will overcome.

DAY 14: KINDNESS

One of my greatest criticisms of churches today is the condemnation rather than compassion people receive. Churches are supposed to be a place where people go to be encouraged, loved and unconditionally accepted but it's often an experience where they are judged, rebuffed and looked down upon. I've never understood the harshness and hypocrisy within many in the religious community because none of us are perfect and we all make different kinds of mistakes.

The story about the Woman At the Well has always been dear to my heart because of how kindly and lovingly Jesus spoke to the woman. Jesus met her while he rested at Jacob's well around noontime, the hottest part of the day, when the woman came alone to draw water. The other women drew their water together, fellowshipping early in the day while it was cooler. The fact that she drew water alone is significant. The other women ostracized her because she was living openly with a man to whom she wasn't married.

She was a Samaritan, a group of people who the Jews felt superior to, so she was shocked when Jesus asked her for some water. After the chatted a few minutes about water and living water, Jesus asked her to call her husband.

When she replied she didn't have a husband, Jesus gently rebuked her and explained who He was and why her behavior was not at His standard. Jesus could've verbally ripped her apart or condemned her to hell – but He didn't. He was kind and loving throughout their encounter at the well.

The compassion and kindness Jesus showed The Woman At the Well is what we should show others. Let this be the day you remember that kindness and compassion are much more effective than condemnation and judgment. Compassion will touch many more people than unkindness ever will.

Today's Affirmation:

I will be kind to others. I recognize that I'm an imperfect person living in an imperfect world.

DAY 15: GOODNESS

Malcolm X is one of the most captivating and intelligent men of his time. He made such an amazing metamorphosis during his seven years of incarceration. He taught himself to read with the dictionary and he studied teachings from the Nation of Islam. His unmistakable charisma and articulate way of speaking his truths made him quite powerful in drawing many followers to the Nation. His talents made him a very influential member and orator, so much so he eventually overshadowed his religious leader's sphere of influence.

All Muslims who can afford to do so are called to make a pilgrimage to Mecca, called the Hajj. Malcolm's Hajj caused another significant life transformation within him because of the people he met and relationships he forged. During his pilgrimage, he met Muslims with blue eyes and blonde hair and these meetings changed and influenced his hopes for and views of positive race relations. He returned to New York with a transformed mind. Malcolm's new perspective widened the already divisive rift between him and the Nation of Islam. His formal separation from the Nation worsened the matter, though he did not become any less devout a Muslim. Tragically, after multiple assassination attempts, Malcolm was murdered at the Audubon Ballroom in Manhattan at only 39 years old. It is impossible not to think of the many accomplishments he would have achieved had his life not been cut so short.

Despite his father's murder when he was six, the mental illness that separated him from his mother, a prison sentence and a separation from the Nation of Islam, Malcolm used his experiences and inner determination to evolve into a man who saw worth and value in everyone. He was a faithful husband and father, a stellar example of a dedicated family man and one of the most brilliant orators in American history. Malcolm came to believe there is goodness among us all, to the credit of his own goodness and concern for others. We can be like Malcolm by looking past our differences and embracing the good in others.

Today's Affirmation:

I will be the best person I can be. I won't stop growing or evolving into the person I'm destined to be.

DAY 16: FAITHFULNESS

One of the most inspiring Christian examples of faithfulness I've ever known is the Woman With the Issue of Blood. This woman hemorrhaged for twelve years without relief. Despite seeing many physicians and healers for treatment, she had not been cured. I cannot imagine how depressed and discouraged she must have been. I know how difficult a patient I can be when I don't feel well over a very short period of time so it's difficult to process how this woman had the determination to persevere through such a protracted illness. When we experience prolonged times of challenge of sadness, we often learn very quickly who our staunchest supporters are. She was probably ostracized by people she once called friends and if she had a husband or significant other, he probably abandoned her too.

The woman probably heard through the grapevine that Jesus was in town. Having heard what a powerful man Jesus was, the woman had deep faith that Jesus could heal her as he had countless other people. Whenever Jesus came to town, there was always a huge crowd and he was closely protected by His disciples so there was no guarantee of getting close to him. The woman wasn't able to speak directly to Jesus to ask for healing but she did manage to touch the bottom of his robe. Jesus felt healing power leave His body so He asked who touched him. The disciples told Him it was impossible to determine who'd touched Him in such a large crowd but Jesus insisted that someone deliberately touched Him.

    The woman came forward and admitted she touched Jesus because she believed He would heal her body. Jesus told her it was her faith that healed and made her whole. No matter what religion you practice, exercise your faith. Believe in the power of your prayers. Know that things will be alright if only because you believe.

Today's Affirmation:

I will believe faithfully. I won't waver or doubt.

DAY 17: HUMILITY

My father taught me that it's always important to live with a spirit of humility. He was right. Great people are always willing to be "little." Their greatness comes from within, from their hearts and willingness to uplift others rather than themselves. Being a gentle person doesn't mean thinking less of oneself, it means thinking of others more. There are countless reasons h is such an important quality. When we have a spirit of humility, we're able to sympathize and empathize well with others in painful times and they can freely rejoice in the best of times. Gentle people feel the pain of others and they don't need to have center stage because their egos prevent them from having a heart for others.

Humble people forgive quickly because they are eternally grateful they're forgiven. They know how valuable they are in God's sight so it's first nature to return the same love and compassion to others. Gentle people are able to love rather than judge and empathize instead of scoffing and rejoicing when other people make mistakes and fall. A humble spirit has a teachable spirit. It's easy for gentle people to realize they aren't omniscient or perfect. They relish the opportunity to learn and develop and share their lessons and growth with others. Humility doesn't take anything away from us but it is a gift that keeps on giving. More importantly, it helps us give freely of ourselves to others. A gentle spirit is the foundation of a happy life.

Think of how you can be a gentler person. Perhaps a friend has made a mistake and they're embarrassed and humiliated. How can you support them in love? Remember how valuable each of us is and how uniquely gifted we are in diverse ways. Use that thought to be gentle and kind with everyone you come into contact with. Your gentle spirit could change someone else's life and it will definitely change yours.

Today's Affirmation:

I am a gentle and loving person. I know that a gentle spirit will enhance all of my relationships with others.

DAY 18: SELF-CONTROL

Everyone loses sometimes but that doesn't make anyone a loser. Our world is obsessed with competition. We learn during childhood that winners are most celebrated and that losers are perceived as weaker and second best. A spirit of competition has its place at a sporting event or during a contest but we must accept that we won't win every time and that we learn powerful lessons from our losses. In life, we must learn to make the best of every negative situation.

Countless historical figures have stood up to power and temporarily lost ground in some situations. Think of Rosa Parks. At 42, she refused to give up her seat on the bus so a white passenger could sit down. Her arrest was a temporary setback but her act of refusal ignited the Montgomery Bus Boycott, a major death knell for Jim Crow laws. Rosa's arrest, a simple act of civil disobedience, is a prime example of winning with renewed strength and a firm purpose.

One of the world's most recognized painters is Leonardo DaVinci. Of his forth most famous paintings, the Mona Lisa is one of the world's most recognized and adored works of art. DaVinci was 51 when he painted the enigmatic and captivating Mona Lisa. Though he began painting much earlier, his most notable works emerged nearly twenty years later. If DaVinci hadn't continued to paint despite his lack of acclaim, the world might never have been beguiled by the Mona Lisa's smile.

Our challenging times teach us graciousness and self-control. Rosa Parks was gracious and used self-control despite being reviled simply for being a black woman who wanted to sit on the bus after a long day of work. Yet, she helped change American history. DaVinci continued to paint despite not receiving immediate acclaim for his work. He did not give up and lose control of his gift or motivation. How will you persevere when you're disappointed? Make it a point to use self-control during the challenging times of your life like Rosa and DaVinci.

Today's Affirmation:

I will always be a winner. No matter how things look, I will believe, control my emotions and overcome.

DAY 19: LOVE

Love never rejoices at injustice and unfairness. Instead, love rejoices when truth, justice and fairness prevail. Our world is full of injustice and simply horrible situations that exist because our world needs love. Love is the only antidote for the hatred that drives the injustice and atrocities plaguing our world.

The Reverend Dr. Martin Luther King, Jr., a Nobel Peace Prize winner, once said, "Darkness cannot drive out darkness, only light can do that. Hate cannot drive out hate, only love can do that." Dr. King dedicated his life to the protest of the second class treatment blacks received in a highly divided nation. His internationally acclaimed I Have A Dream speech was a call to action for the end of racism and it called for equal civil and economic rights for all people. His lifetime work and protests were pivotal to the American Civil Rights Movement.

Dr. Elie Wiesel, a Holocaust survivor, won a Nobel Peace Prize for his work. He wrote books and scholarly articles about his experiences and spoke all over the world, sharing his firsthand knowledge of the dangers of hatred and oppression. The horrors and abuse he experienced in Nazi concentration camps inspired Dr. Wiesel to remain heavily involved in Jewish causes and he was one of the most vocal supporters of the US Holocaust Memorial Museum in Washington, DC. His life's mission was opposing, speaking out and eliminating human suffering and the atrocities committed against all racial groups.

      Dr. King and Dr. Wiesel loved their fellow man. Instead of becoming bitter as a result of the mistreatment they experienced, each used their sadness positively by speaking out and helping others. Our world needs more people to love others enough to work tirelessly so truth and justice prevail. What are you willing to do to make your community a better place? Let this be the day we talk less and act more to bring about justice and equality in our world.

Today's Affirmation:

I will love others and rejoice when justice and truth prevail.
I will do what I can to fight injustice in my community.

DAY 20: JOY

Things aren't always as bad as they seem and they are always better when we focus on the positives. One of the best ways to live a joyful life is to be happy and to maintain good spirits. It isn't always easy to do but focusing on our positive provides us with the blessing to recognize how good things really are. There are times we will all suffer. Our difficult times teach us to persevere and be resilient. Resilience in challenging times helps us build the strength in character that builds us up. Strength in character gives us hope and the ability to focus on and believe in the possibilities awaiting us in the future.

Stephen King is one of my favorite authors. Though he has sold more than 350 million copies of his works and numerous of his works have become motion pictures, he wasn't an overnight success. Publishers rejected his work at least thirty times, leading him to put his first novel in the garbage. His wife Tabitha rescued the manuscript from the trash can and pushed him to press on. If she hadn't encouraged him to see the brighter side and hold onto his joy as a creator and writer, American literature wouldn't have benefitted from King's influence.

The things we're passionate about bring us great joy and we can't allow anyone to take that feeling from us.

Things won't always be easy so we have to hold onto the happiness we feel when working with our passions. When we find something that brings us joy, we have to appreciate it and remain dedicated to all of its possibilities. Things won't always be easy but they'll always be worthwhile when we concentrate on how happy they make us.

     Feel true joy through your passions. If it's positive and adds to your happiness, don't let anything stand in your way. Life is too short not to live and achieve to your highest potential.

Today's Affirmation:

I will live a joy-filled life. No one and nothing will steal my joy.

DAY 21: PEACE

No matter how hard we try to find people, material possessions and events to help us create or hold onto our peace, our peace never comes from outside sources. We are responsible for holding onto our peace. Peacefulness is truly an inside job.

One of the most important Christian figures from whom we can learn a valuable lesson about inner peace is The Apostle Paul. In one of his most significant writings to Philippi, Paul told the people he learned to be content in every situation whether he had a little or a lot. He learned not to rely on external circumstances or his financial standing for happiness and peace. What a wonderful conclusion to use as a guiding principle for a happy life.

The Apostle Paul faced many challenging experiences throughout his lifetime, especially once he became a Christian. He was bitten by a poisonous snake. He was persecuted for his beliefs and once imprisoned in a cell where he was waist deep in sewage waste. Yet, he did not allow any of these events to disturb his peace or chip away at his beliefs.

Peace comes in great measure when we are able to remain content and grateful in every situation. We cannot control the outcome of every challenge we face but we can control our attitudes and state of mind while experiencing life's challenges. No matter what challenges we face, we can endure them with a positive attitude and the faith that things will work out as they should rather than how we expect or insist that they should be. There is great strength in being content at all times rather than being anxious about every situation, especially those we cannot control.

Let this be the day you decided to set your mind and be content despite what you are facing. Be at peace in all that you do and in how you react. There is no greater blessing than contentment and inner peace.

Today's Affirmation:

I will remain at peace. I'm determined to be content at all times.

DAY 22: PATIENCE

Some of our biggest challenges are our most difficult and we will only overcome them with patience. One of the most patient people I've ever heard of is Joseph. He lived a life that was an exercise of patience and inner strength. Joseph's brother sold him into slavery. Potiphar, a powerful Egyptian, purchased Joseph to work in his home. Joseph worked diligently and became the head servant. Potiphar's wife became attracted to Joseph and propositioned him sexually. Joseph consistently rebuffed her advances and fell into a honey trap one day when he and Potiphar's wife were alone. After he routinely refused her advances, she grabbed his coat, pulling him closer, but he quickly left the room, leaving his coat behind. The rejection enraged her enough to falsely accused Joseph of attacking her and Joseph went to prison.

Sitting in his cell, Joseph must have wondered what would happen next. He found favor with the warden and became his assistant. When Pharaoh sent two of his officers to jail for offending him, they each had vivid dreams Joseph interpreted. After interpreting the first man's dream, Joseph asked him to appeal to Pharaoh for his release. The second man's dream didn't have a favorable outcome. After Pharaoh freed the first man from prison, the man forgot about Joseph for two years until

Pharaoh had a dream that needed interpretation. Once Joseph interpreted the dream, he became Pharaoh's right hand, eventually saving Egypt from famine and welcoming and saving the brothers who sold him into slavery years before.

      Joseph endured a string of heartbreaks that would have crushed many of us. It was his patience and faith in God that allowed him to conquer his obstacles and thrive despite adverse circumstances. Being patient helps us survive in the bleakest of times when we're ready to surrender our hope. Use your inner strength and patience to overcome and thrive in your challenging times too.

Today's Affirmation:

I will be patient when things don't go the way I want them to go. I believe all things happen for me, not to me.

DAY 23: KINDNESS

We will have disagreements with other people. It's inevitable. What we don't have to do is be prideful and refuse to apologize or forgive. How many times have we had a disagreement with someone and held grudges, refusing to forgive? How many relationships have suffered or been ruined as a result? We cannot allow pride and the roots of bitterness to ruin our happiness and relationships. I've known some people who held eternal grudges but were unable to remember why they were angry in the first place.

In truth, the amount of love or forgiveness we show others is crucial. First, we should treat others with kindness as we want to be treated. When we offend someone we care about, we want to be forgiven. What if we offend someone and they refuse to forgive us? I had a chat with a dear friend who resents the phrase " Be the bigger person." Being the bigger person doesn't come from a place of pride. It comes from knowing that someone has to make the first move and being humble enough to be that person. I believe we each have to be the bigger person sometimes because we value the person we argued or disagreed with more than we care about being right. That's kindness and love in action.

Kind people have tender hearts because they value people and their feelings. Look for opportunities to show kindness and love. Joseph certainly did. He forgave the brothers who sold him into slavery and greeted them with kindness, forgiveness and love when he had every right to be angry. You can show others kindness and love when they hurt you too. It isn't always easy to show kindness to those who've hurt and mistreated us but it's always the right response. Our world certainly needs more kindness. Make this the day you become determined to show kindness as a natural response. It won't always be easy but you can set your mind to do so.

Today's Affirmation:

I will be kind to others and humble myself when necessary to heal and nurture my relationships.

DAY 24: GOODNESS

Mother Teresa, an Albanian nun and missionary, was one of the mightiest people who worked for the hopes of others. When she founded the Missionaries of Charity, it changed the direction of her life. She touched lives all over the world through medical treatment, food, counseling and other acts of love and compassion. It wasn't an easy road for her. In the earlier days of fulfilling her purpose, Mother Teresa became a beggar. I believe her direct experiences with poverty made her all the more compassionate and determined to help others.

A vivid memory about a former student comes to mind. In one of the schools where I served as principal, one of my students eagerly approached me and asked if we could support a well known charity by collecting shoes for less-fortunate children. This charity provides shoes for children all over the world. In some cases, the charity provides the first pair of shoes the children have owned. He believed a school-wide effort would be successful. His earnest desire to help others touched my heart and renewed my hope. During this shoe drive, he displayed his leadership skills by speaking to the other students and encouraging them to participate and make a difference among other children. The shoe drive was a success and a tribute to his heart for others. It also made a significant difference among the children who received shoes and love from other children.

There are people we can help, love and show goodness every day. Too many of us think that we can't help others enough as significantly as we would like to through small acts of kindness and love but every effort counts. We might not touch global lives at the scale Mother Teresa did but we can make the lives of those close to us better like my student did with our school's shoe project. Whether it's a idea on a grand scale or something small and personal, never let an opportunity to show goodness from your heart go to waste.

Today's Affirmation:

I will be helpful to others when the opportunity presents itself. No act of goodness is too small if it makes a difference in someone's life.

DAY 25: FAITHFULNESS

It's easy for friends to be faithful during the happiest and prosperous of times. People are at their most agreeable when we have much to give. That's when it's easy to appreciate our friends. When the negative times come, when we're traveling our rockiest paths or when we have a substantial loss, those are the moments we often glimpse the truest feelings people have toward us. Think of the Prodigal Son. When he loosely spent his premature inheritance, he was surrounded by friends. Once his money was gone, so were his friends. He had nowhere to live except the pigpen. As he ate out of a pig's trough, he was alone wearing rags and stinking as badly as his animal companions. People flock around us while we're abounding but we learn quickly who's in our corner when we're abased.

Several personal tragedies taught me quite well the difference between my true friends and friendships based on convenience and self-interest. My difficult times also introduced me to new friends who came into my life when I had nothing to offer except friendship. I have no resentment for the lessons I've learned about friendship. The lessons benefitted me in several ways. I learned to be led by reason rather than my ego. People are human and sometimes the things they do aren't personally directed to us but a part of what they're going through. I've learned in Technicolor that everyone isn't trustworthy. Sometimes the very person who you believed was most in your corner was never loyal. Most of all, I learned to be the kind of friend who remains constant and loving through the best and worst of times. We can't expect people to show us love and faithfulness when we aren't giving those things ourselves.

Today, set your mind to be a faithful friend in every circumstance. Be the friend you want your friends to be to you. Decide to be a ray of sunshine and consistency in a bleak, ever changing world.

Today's Affirmation:

I will be a trustworthy person. My loved ones can count on me to be there for them in good and bad times.

DAY 26: HUMILITY

Have you ever been around someone who talked about themselves constantly and makes every conversation about them? It is a daunting task to have an open conversation or meaningful relationship with prideful people who are determined to keep the spotlight on themselves. It's often a frustrating feeling because it's difficult to connect with people who show no interest in who we are, what we're feeling and what we've experienced.

The depth of a person's humility and capacity to allow others to shine shows how deeply they are able to love. People with humble spirits build one another up. They realize everyone has something of value to offer and they give others the opportunity to contribute to conversations and to the relationship. Humble people also change the conversation when others are being ripped apart. If they can't change the conversation, they leave it because they think of how the person being gossiped about would feel.

Humble, gracious people are able to build other people up when they're hurting because they've often experienced deeply painful circumstances of their own. Our deep hurts and heartbreaks enable us to connect to as empathetic, kindred spirits on a much deeper level than merely "doing what's right." The connection to other people's pain helps the humble person think of others more than they do themselves at the time. Most importantly, humility and kindness heals wounds and breaks barriers among people.

Let this be the day we begin to think more about how others feel. Let's become more curious about their opinions and qualities. It's time to connect with others on a deeper level. It will make people around you happier and grateful for your friendship and transform your spirit to a higher level of humility and love.

Today's Affirmation:

I will look at others through humility today. It's an important part of relationship building.

DAY 27: SELF-CONTROL

When people bring little tidbits of "intel" about others, rest assured they likely gossip to the next person about you. Don't encourage them with do tell and an eager ear. Be as cautious about what you listen to as you are about what you say. We have an obligation to believe the best of others. In order to do so, we have to control our eagerness to listen to, repeat and initiate gossip.

Our modern rapid communication is a blessing and a curse. Social media forums like Facebook, Instagram and Twitter allow us to communicate instantly. Social media has reshaped the way we convey information and its influence often reshapes our thoughts. Instant communication can be a wonderful thing but if we share at the height of angry or hurtful emotions, we won't use social media wisely. At the height of our emotions we aren't always sure about the accuracy of what we're saying because we are being reactionary.

How many of us have posted passive-aggressive or accusatory rants in a heated moment without verifying facts or pausing to take a deep breath? Such passionate and heated arguments abound on social media and it takes self-control not to engage. Where is the action that would make a difference? When an argument surfaces on your or a friend's timeline, focus on the positive tangible actions you can take. Move beyond lip service, wasted energy and virtual debates.

It's no different when friends and loved ones come to us with information about other people. How many times have our listening ears willingly listened to and allowed ourselves to be influenced without knowing the facts of a situation? It's imperative for us to use self-control and think for ourselves when it comes to what we believe. Be determined to make solid decisions and informed opinions.

Today's Affirmation:

I will think for myself. I won't jump to conclusions.

DAY 27: LOVE

A pet peeve that turns me off more than most things is a person who readily talks about how much they love God while they squander so many opportunities to love and uplift others by helping them when they're in need. They don't love people through difficult times or show them grace and mercy when they need it. It's easy to talk about how much we love God and others but so much more powerful to show our love through what we do. As the adage goes, our actions speak much more loudly than our words.

The story about Jesus and the woman caught in adultery reminds us of how important it is to love people through our actions and show love in difficult situations. I can imagine the prideful countenance of the men who hauled this woman into the temple. What an eager lynch mob they were. They reminded Jesus how the old laws required the woman to be stoned, asking Him what He thought should happen.

This is a powerful story for several reasons. The group is trying to put Jesus on the spot to condemn the woman without all of the facts. Second, and perhaps most significantly, their actions expose the judgmental, unkind nature of the religious leaders. Jesus reminded the group how hypocritical it is for one sinner to judge another.

How often do we judge others by their shortcomings while ignoring our own? How often do we feel rejected when people judge us by their shortcomings? A hypocritical, prideful attitude prevents us from loving others without reservation and it prevents us from having loving relationships. Love is made of grace and mercy. Let's be sure to love others with graceful, merciful and forgiving hearts that show them how we feel because that's certainly what we want them do to for us.

Today's Affirmation:

I will be a loving person. The love I have for others will show through my actions.

DAY 28: JOY

My Uncle Harold passed away recently and it was an enormous loss for my family. He was a giant in my eyes because of his immense kindness and forgiving spirit and because of his ability to live a life of true joy. Uncle Harold was very much a person who embraced life and the struggles he faced with face and a beautiful heart. He was a person who made you feel loved and appreciated just by being in his presence. One of his favorite songs was *His Eye Is On the Sparrow*, a very fitting song to describe the spirit of joy and love in such a wonderful person.

Civilla Martin wrote the song's inspiring lyrics in 1905 because of the influence of a couple with whom she and her husband developed a close friendship. This couple didn't have an easy life. One was bedridden and the other was handicapped. Despite their circumstances, both were always a joy to everyone who spent time with them. When Martin's husband pointed out to the couple how optimistic, caring and full of joy they were, the wife responded that God's eyes tenderly watched the sparrows so she was positive God watched over her.

How touching and appropriate that *His Eye Is On the Sparrow* was born of the joy this couple showed others despite their circumstances. Uncle Harold was such a person too and the enormity of his beautiful spirit inspires me to remember to make the effort to be present in every moment and to spread joy among others with every opportunity. How blessed I was to have an uncle like him as an example of joy and love.

Seek every opportunity you can to be a beacon of joy and love to others. You never know how much your being a joy to be around will improve their lives and add to their happiness. Joy makes our lives more worthwhile through every circumstance. Invest in the happiness of others. It's a gift that never stops giving because you will be encouraged just by bringing joy to the lives of others. Spread joy wherever you go!!

Today's Affirmation:

I will be joyful in every circumstance and bring joy to the lives of others.

DAY 29: PEACE

Holding grudges drains our energy. Just as it takes more muscles to frown than to smile, it takes enormous amounts of energy to be angry. Forgiveness is a gift we also give ourselves. Yet, so many of us scowl, frown and withhold forgiveness from others instead of realizing how much happier and more productive we would be if we let go of our egos and chose peace, love and happiness instead.

Someone will always use, hurt and offend us. It's a part of human nature to err but as Alexander Pope said, to forgive is divine. We cannot move on with our lives and become all we are capable of and destined to be with unforgiving spirits. When we hold on to grudges and offenses, we're holding on to negativity and bad memories. Life has too many blessings and beautiful moments for us to savor to miss them because we refuse to let go of the bad times. Why allow the bad tastes to sour the sweeter moments? When someone has hurt us and we hold on to hurt and angry feelings, it's almost like insisting we are owed something for our pain and suffering. Forgiveness opens the door to a happier, more fulfilling life and the possibility of reconciliation.

It used to be difficult for me to forgive others at times and I made myself unhappier in the process of holding grudges. I robbed myself of peace and joy because of my pride and desire to be right. Eventually, when I needed forgiveness for a major mistake in my life, I realized my inner peace greatly outweighed my need to be right and I remembered how important it is for me to forgive others who'd wronged me.

When we forgive and move forward, we hold on to our joy and inner peace. Grudges are like a ticking hand grenade. That's why we must release them before they destroy us. Choose to forgive those who have hurt you. Let this be the day your inner peace matters more than holding on to the worst moments. Choose to move forward.

Today's Affirmation:

I will remain at peace. I won't jeopardize my peace by holding grudges.

DAY 30: PATIENCE

Impatience is one of the most destructive human traits. It often prevents us from doing the best we can where we are at the moment when we feel anxious or pressed to move forward. It makes us ungrateful for what we have because we become overly focused on what we want. Impatience causes us to fixate on the outcomes we want and it clouds our judgment and discernment. Sometimes we need to stop for a moment and patiently pay attention to what's going on around us. We have to learn to pause long enough to understand what *is* before we decide it's wrong or seek to change it.

We must focus on the positive people, the ones who show love and support while giving the harsh truth when we need it. They tell the truth in love because they want us to feel the value of patience and nurturing when we need their support. Value those who stay to fuel us with love and support when everyone else leaves us behind because they were patient enough not to leave when we needed them most. We must be grateful for the ones who didn't throw us to the wolves. They were a shining example of how to treat others.

We need to be the most patient with others when we're upset with them or involved in a situation that frustrates us. The experiences we've endured and overcome are a pathway to our purpose because they teach us the value of patience as we grow. Our disappointments enable us to use our deepest pain for the greater good and prepare us to show patience and love to others when they need us most. We become the example they need to see. Focus on negative forces and the things that upset and agitate you only long enough to remove, block or eliminate them. Once you're past those things, let them stay in your rear view mirror while you focus on what's ahead of you with a valuable lesson about patience in your arsenal.

Today's Affirmation:

I will be patient and wait when it's necessary. Rushing doesn't help me, it only distracts me.

DAY 31: KINDNESS

One of the happiest sounds we share with one another is laughter. Yet, we must all do better when it comes to sharing love and compassion and supporting one another through the tough times. It's easy to spend time with one another when we're happy. It's when we're burdened and sad that love and compassion from others is sorely needed and most meaningful.

While waiting for a doctor's appointment not long ago, I flipped through a magazine and read an old story about Zach Galifianakis. Because I enjoyed the Hangover movies and Alan's antics so much, the article caught my attention. Galifianakis is the epitome of kindness in action. For the Hangover III premiere, his guest was an elderly woman he met years before. This woman used to work at a laundromat Galifianakis patronized. Since they met, the woman experienced financial difficulties that caused her to become homeless.

Once he heard about her financial challenges, Galifianakis paid the lease for an apartment for her. As an added bonus, his friend and fellow celebrity Renee Zellweger furnished the apartment. What a blessing for a woman who was down and out, who like felt the prisoner of a hopeless situation! Imagine what would happen if each of us helped others in the same way that are in need.

You're probably thinking that most people don't have the financial backing to help someone as deeply as did Galifianakis and Zellweger. It would be an amazing world if we could. However, loving and helping others with kindness doesn't always have to be on a grand scale. An act of kindness of any size is always an appropriate action. Buying groceries for friends who are struggling or donating a case of cold water to a thirsty construction crew working in the heat is just as kind and helpful. As long as we help others, humanity will thrive because of love and compassion.

Today's Affirmation:

I will be generous with others by being kind. I don't have to be financially wealthy to help others, just rich in kindness.

DAY 32: GOODNESS

One individual can't overcome evil with a single act of goodness but collectively, our acts of goodness can change the world. Multiple incidences of goodness provide a foundation we can build on and expand. A story my mother used to read me, *Why the Chimes Rang* by Raymond MacDonald Alden, reminds me how the tiniest bits of good can overwhelm and change the world.

In this story, two brothers journeyed to the cathedral to attend Christmas services and to give their gift. As they got closer to the city, they noticed an older woman who urgently needed their help. Pedro, the eldest, decided to stay with the woman until she was well enough to move despite the fact that he desperately wanted to make the trip too. He gave his little brother his offering, a piece of silver, to place on the altar.

It was well known that the cathedral's bells only rang when a heartfelt offering was placed on the altar. When the time to present offering came, many people gave various gifts, most of which were resplendent and opulent. Not one chime rang. Imagine how the worshippers gasped when the king put his crown, a bejeweled crown of great worth, on the altar without any chimes ringing. Soon after, the chimes began to ring after little brother put Pedro's small piece of silver on the altar.

When we do our best to help others and give from our hearts, our world changes for the better each time. It doesn't take huge donations or gifts, grandiose efforts or public ceremony to help others. Giving large donations or gifts is wonderful but it's what we do with love and compassion that are most effective. The things we do from the heart are what mean most and what matter most.

Today's Affirmation:

I will dedicate myself to giving my best to others in need. It isn't how much I give but my attitude while I'm giving that means the most.

DAY 33: FAITHFULNESS

Our world has become increasingly volatile and untrustworthy. Too many of our leaders speak fluent doublespeak and won't own up to it when they're exposed. They waver when we need leadership most and are no longer guided by the principles of faithfulness and sincerity to their constituents. We, in apathy and disgust, don't hold them as accountable as we should when we have every right to expect them to say what they mean, mean what they say and act as they've promised to. It's a two-pronged problem that affects every branch of government and community. Both sides have dropped the ball. We must be more faithful to one another and our principles in order to improve our communities and quality of life. Our leaders must be more scrupulous and faithful to doing what's best for us rather than themselves.

Countless promises are made during election seasons but rarely kept for several reasons. Too many of our leaders will say anything to win. Second, they don't keep most of their promises and use all manner of excuses when they don't. Third, too many special interest groups control what happens for the average American citizen. Our leaders accept so many campaign contributions they become beholden to special interests rather than what's best for the people who elect them.

Everything we do and say leaves an imprint. Our words and actions reveal who we are at the core. The way we treat others and what we do says more about us than anything else before we ever speak a word. Kindness, goodness and other positive virtues mean more than anything else, but if we're not faithful to our virtues, our action won't mean much. Until we can learn to be confident enough to be true to ourselves, faithful enough to do what we say we'll do and until we hold our elected officials accountable to do the same, our society won't improve.

Today's Affirmation:

I will remain stable and steady. People can depend on me to be faithful to what I say.

DAY 34: HUMILITY

It takes considerable strength to treat people with kindness when they've been cruel toward us. It's even more difficult when you've been abused as a child because a cold, indifferent adult resents you just because you're there. My Uncle Harold, a man I loved and respected with an immeasurable depth, overcame a childhood teeming with maltreatment and unkindness, and he became one of the best men I've ever known.

His mother died during childbirth so he never had the opportunity to know her, hear her voice or see her smile. His father, my paternal grandfather, married my grandmother when Uncle Harold was a young boy. My grandmother, a cold selfish woman, was concerned with appearances. She wanted to appear as pious to others, yet she was neither kind, nurturing or loving toward Uncle Harold. She was so hateful, she only allowed him to spend one summer with his father. She lied on him frequently during that summer, causing him to get whippings for things he didn't do. Otherwise, she ignored him as if he wasn't there.

I cannot imagine how he felt as a child who was mistreated for no reason but I know her cruelty and unkind manner deeply affected him. He didn't become angry or vengeful when he was an adult. He forgave her and treated her as if she hadn't been the proverbially evil stepmother she indeed was. His ability to forgive her primal abuse, behavior that would incite most people to behave in a retaliatory way, has always amazed me. He knew how to be a gentle spirit and stand tall in a situation that would break many people. His example has always inspired me, so much so that I think of his enduring and beautiful spirit when I need to be humbly strong.

Aspire to be strong when someone else's unkindness seeks to weaken your spirit. Let this be the day you recognize a humble spirit trumps a prideful one.

Today's Affirmation:

I will be a gentle person. My humility makes me strong because I know how it feels to be mistreated.

DAY 35: SELF-CONTROL

The most adverse times we experience build character and prepare us to be successful in any situation. I lost a job in extremely unfair circumstances. I felt defeated. The unjust events broke my heart and for a period of time, I became bitter and depressed. There were times I wanted to surrender to the despair. Had it not been for the love of my parents and a few other angels, I wouldn't have had the will to survive.

Once I began to heal, I realize the times I spent grappling with adversity redefined me as a woman and as a believer. Adversity planted a deeper seed of strength in my heart and mind that made me determined to not only survive but to thrive. I dug into my roots like a palm tree. Palm trees bend completely in winds of 200 mph but they don't break. Once the turbulence ends, palms bounce right back to an upright position. When you're enduring a test, behave like a palm tree.

The most revealing thing about adversity is that it's an invaluable teaching experience about who we are at our core. Overcoming adversity helps us focus on becoming stronger, more prepared survivors in future adverse times. In response to the hurricane of unemployment and unhappiness in my life, I realized *after* the experience, once the storm and winds passed, that I was stronger than I'd ever believed. I developed the resilience of a palm tree.

You are stronger and more like a palm tree than you think. Think of the challenges you've overcome. Your survival rate is one hundred percent and you're stronger because of adversity. The next time winds blow in your life and a storm seems to rage without relenting, remember that you might be affected as you endure the storm but that as soon as the turbulence stops, you'll be stronger than ever too!

Today's Affirmation:

I will be victorious because I'm as resilient as a palm tree.
I bend but I don't break.

DAY 36: LOVE

When we first fall in love, we can't stop thinking about the one we love. We grin helplessly like Cheshire Cats at the thought of the person. We smile uncontrollably when we see them. A special song reminds us of them. Hugs and kisses make us feel warm and tingly. We can't do enough kind things to show our devotion. Yet, so many romantic relationships end because we stop doing the affectionate things we did at the beginning. Sometimes we're not as caring because of an argument or disagreement we have a difficult time letting go of. Perhaps one partner is going through something and isn't as loving as usual and the other person feels weighed upon. Maybe one person feels unappreciated and becomes resentful and, rather than expressing their feelings, they hold it in, hoping the other person will change.

Falling in love doesn't mean our work is done when it comes to building and strengthening love. Love means giving without worrying about who's giving the most. True love never gives up, it's relentless. True love remains faithful and constant. It endures every circumstance. Why do so many of us struggle to romantically love this way?

A story I once heard illustrates how people often drift apart. A married couple had drifted apart. The wife felt the distance and told her husband how she felt, reminding him how when they were dating how they sat so closely in the car that people often couldn't tell if whether they were the same person. Smiling slyly, the husband reminded his wife he was still driving and that he hadn't moved.

What a gentle, thought-provoking reminder of how important it is to continue doing the things, however small or endearing we did when we first fell in love. Never stop nurturing and building love. Instead of concentrating on who's doing more in the relationship, be so busy loving the other person that you remain as close as when you first fell in love.

Today's Affirmation:

I will be a loving person who nurtures all of my relationships with kindness and consistency.

DAY 37: JOY

We have a tendency to focus tightly on what we've lost. It's human nature to think about it and it's not always easy to overcome loss and disappointment. However, it's more beneficial for us to train our minds to focus on what we have left. When we view life through a negative lens, we drain our joy and the joy of those around us, but when we dwell on the positives we're blessed to have, we hold onto our joy.

Sidney Poitier, a Bahamian American, certainly must have been discouraged after his first audition when the casting director told him he should become a dishwasher rather than wasting time becoming an actor. Instead of being angry or sinking into a pit of self-pity, Sidney chose to focus on his talent and hold on to hope. With an attitude driven by hope and a spirit of perseverance, he became the first Bahamian and the first black man to win an Academy Award for Best Actor. He also won numerous other awards, including but not limited to the Presidential Medal of Freedom, a Golden Globe and the Golden Globe Cecil B. DeMille Award, an honorary Oscar and a SAG Lifetime Achievement Award. What if Sidney had given up because of one ill advised opinion and become a dishwasher? He chose to remain hopeful and pursue his dream.

Had Sidney not held onto his joy and enthusiasm for acting and lost his determination to share his gift with the world, we would never have had the pleasure of enjoying his acting and many humanitarian acts. He chose to hold on to his faith, joy and determination to succeed. Never surrender your joy or hope based on anything in the past or what someone says to you. If you have a dream, live it in technicolor. Work hard to accomplish the goals that will make your dream come true. Believe in your vision and pursue it relentlessly. Focus on the present and pay attention to your blessings you have instead of what you've lost.

Today's Affirmation:

I will focus on what makes me happy and I won't allow challenges to steal my joy.

DAY 38: PEACE

People will irritate us at times. Perhaps they've slighted or offended us. Maybe we don't agree with their opinions. Maybe we think they'd be better off if they thought or acted more like we do. What we often forget is how we might irritate, slight or offend others too. Someone will always say or do something that offends us but we don't have to give them the power to disturb our inner peace. We can choose to behave like royals and bring people into our peace instead.

Life is a series of lessons we must master. We will continue to experience similar events and the same kinds of frustration until we learn what we're meant to learn about them and about ourselves. We won't always get closure after our disappointments. We have to be at peace with that too. Sometimes things just end without an obvious reason or purpose at that time. We have to pay attention, wise up and pass the test. Then we're prepared to move on to the next lesson.

Another way we can have more peace in our lives is to look for the good in others and accept them as they are. By doing so, we often discover the best in ourselves. We will achieve more peace by accepting people rather than trying to change them. Have you seen the best in others lately? Have you looked for it? We can also expect others to look for the best in us and accept us as we are. We don't have to be less of who we are so others will accept us. We will be at peace by unapologetically being ourselves. There are people who will appreciate us as we are and we can enjoy peaceful relationships with those people. If we want peace, we may have to end our relationships with the people who don't accept us as we are.

We can either fight life and every disappointment we experience or we can accept things as lessons. Remembering that things happen *for us* rather than to us is a way to live in peace.

Today's Affirmation:

I will be at peace with who other people are. I don't have the right to change anyone.

DAY 39: PATIENCE

Albert Einstein is one of the most brilliant scientists in our world's history, yet he wasn't always so highly regarded. In fact, he showed signs of developmental delays. He didn't talk until he was four years old and he didn't begin reading until he was seven. Albert was antisocial and this was of great concern to his parents and teachers. Multitalented, Albert became an accomplished violinist and he had a natural proficiency with mathematics and science because they intrigued him. He was particularly fond of geometry and he mastered calculus by the time he was sixteen. He dropped out of school because he was bored but finished his education once he began attending the Swiss Federal Polytechnic Institute.

Albert Einstein, a man who didn't start speaking as early as most children do, changed the face of physics and he won a Nobel Peace Prize among many other honors. He presented ideas many people have a difficult time mastering at his level. The greatest physicist in the world was once unwanted by some of his professors but once he wrote his most famous papers, the academic community created a frenzy when they all lobbied for his services.

Albert was a visionary. Visionaries don't concern themselves with how people view or perceive them. They continue believing in themselves while working diligently to bring their ideas to life. Eventually, they open the eyes of those around them. The delays you're facing are not a denial, they're simply a training ground for the higher ground you're going to and an important installment in your life's story. You will look back on the difficult times when you're living your dream and the delays will one day make sense. If anything, allow your delays and challenges to encourage you to push even harder to achieve your dreams. Don't close the book or stop believing things will work out as they should for you. Turn the page and continue writing your next chapter. Be patient with yourself so you can be visionary in the way you're meant to be!

Today's Affirmation:

I will be a visionary and add something unique to the world. My future is brighter than any of my doubts or delays.

DAY 40: KINDNESS

It's often easy to recognize people who are in pain. We can see it in their eyes and the expressions on their faces. Most of the time, we take the time to talk to people to encourage and motivate them with positive affirmations like "Keep the faith" and "I'll pray for you." There's nothing wrong with encouraging people. It's what kind people do when they realize someone is in pain and or struggling with something. When people are hurting, we can't stop at telling them to take it to God. True compassion means that once we're aware of someone's pain, we become moved to help them relieve and overcome the pain.

Boaz, a biblical character, recognized the struggle Ruth experienced as a young widow. Boaz extended deep kindness to Ruth not only because her beauty captured his attention but also because he heard about her devotion to her mother in law Naomi. Naomi was Boaz's relative. Ruth could have returned to her homeland once her husband died but her compassion and dedication wouldn't allow her to leave Naomi after her husband and both of her sons died, leaving Naomi alone in the world.

Eventually, Ruth and Boaz married. Boaz could have allowed Ruth to live in poverty. However, he decided to pull her up and improve her life. We can look at this story as a guide on how to treat others. There's an essential question we should ask ourselves each day. Do I push people down of do I pull people up? Some of the toughest times of my live have clearly shown me who was there to pull me up. Their compassion for me saved my life from a broken spirit and heart. Their compassion makes me aspire to be a person who pulls others up too.

Will you aspire to pull people up? Look for ways to be kind and compassionate that go beyond lip service. Feel people's pain and take every step to relieve their pain when you can. You can make a difference that could mean everything to someone.

Today's Affirmation:

I will take action and help people overcome their challenges with kindness and compassion.

DAY 41 : GOODNESS

Talk is cheap but actions are a marathon of proof. It's easy to talk about how well we would behave toward people who've wronged us in hypothetical situations or to scold friends we've witnessed acting angrily toward others when the consequences aren't ours to live. What really shows goodness is when we are able to behave agreeably with a person who has just cursed us out for filth. It's also an example of goodness to comfort a friend who's been mistreated because it encourages them to show their goodness to someone in need in the future.

Our character is the essence of who we are. Goodness is the compassionate spirit within us that guides us to do the right thing even when it's difficult to do. We each have good qualities and we do good deeds but the goodness we develop comes solely from God. Christians are supposed to be examples of His goodness, just as other faiths look to the goodness within their gods and beliefs for guidance.

So … what does it mean, then, to be good? Acting fairly with and toward others is an example of showing goodness. Being honest with others is a way to demonstrate goodness. We're called to be the salt of the earth. We should live our lives in such a way that we're seasoning the lives of everyone around us with the best of ourselves.

Compassion, a quality our world sorely needs, is another example of how we can show goodness. Everyone makes mistakes and we know goodness in action when people show us kindness and love especially when we don't truly deserve it. We feel it through forgiveness when people love us enough to forgo revenge. Become and show the sense of fairness and compassion hurting people so desperately need. Let the goodness within you shine brightly to the best of our ability through all you do.

Today's Affirmation:

I will be a lighthouse of goodness for others through what I say and do.

DAY 42: FAITHFULNESS

We learn and grow most when we experience trials, setbacks and discomfort, though these are the times we least enjoy. We all experience pain. We have to be wise enough to allow our pain to push us forward rather than imprisoning us in pits of self-pity. One positive action is the first step toward undoing 99 missteps and it takes faith to believe we can move forward and live brighter lives. We must be faithful enough to realize our failures are a springboard of growth and development. Hope is a significant part of faithfulness because we're staking our hopes on someone bigger than we are. Faithfulness means we believe strongly in something other than ourselves.

In order to take that first step when we're experiencing difficult times, we have to learn from the past without dwelling on it. Our futures are ahead of us, not behind us. We learn vital lessons that prepare us for the future, not to trap us in sad times. We must exercise our faith by looking ahead with hope to brighter days where we can use the knowledge we've gained.

The story of Job is one of the best examples of faith I've heard. Job lost his family and all of his livestock. He continued to believe. His wife wanted him to curse God and die. His friends blamed him for all of the negative things that happened to him. He continued believing. He became ill and developed boils all over his body. I'm sure he had moments of doubt, though he held on to his hope. Job overcame his trials and received twice what he'd lost as a reward for his faith.

Think of failure and success as opposing walls. The only way we will achieve our successes is by knocking down the walls of failure and relentlessly never giving up. It takes time and hard work but we'll never get there if we give up. Keep trying. Keep pushing. Keep the faith. You will make it as long as you refuse to give up.

Today's Affirmation:

I will be successful by using the lessons from my past to become the best person I can be.

DAY 43: HUMILITY

No matter how good a person we intend to be, we are human and we will need correction at some point. It's a real deterrent to our growth if we can't accept correction. There will also be someone we have to correct in a non-offensive, kind manner. What is really important that we never become so arrogant that we cannot receive advice or counsel. Pride, a lack of humility, will block our blessings and cause us to fail too, often a very rapid and hard fall.

Recently, my trainer Hammed had a talk with me that didn't make me happy at the time. He told me I needed to concentrate on my workouts instead of sacrificing them to complete the many other things I was doing, including editing my manuscript for this book. Fuming, I was angry with him all day until I got over myself and realized he was telling me exactly what I needed to hear. That talk we had was pivotal because it put me back on a trajectory where I'm getting stronger, healthier and leaner and it's made a huge difference in my life.

When we're able to give and receive correction with grace and mercy, incredible things happen. First, we benefit from the correction we receive. If we aren't able to receive correction, we won't grow. A humble person acts on correction rather than reacting to it and uses the lesson to his or her benefit. Humble people are also able to start over and move forward after mistakes. They not only recognize how vital second chances are but they also readily give second chances to others. Failure isn't a permanent situation and humble people realize their mistakes aren't their identity, they're a trampoline. They know they can jump to greatness from their mistakes.

Every negative in our lives becomes a positive with the right amount of time, patience and humility. Let this be the day we become strong enough to receive correction and humble enough to use it for our good and the good of others.

Today's Affirmation:

I will be humble enough to receive correction and view it as a blessing. Correction helps me grow and improve.

DAY 43: SELF-CONTROL

One of the most difficult struggles most of us have is controlling our emotions. We have to decide very carefully what deserves our energy and what doesn't. If it isn't productive or edifying or if it disturbs us, we must hold onto our peace.

David was one of the most gifted Bible characters. A young shepherd with older brothers who teased him, he was unassuming and accustomed to spending a lot of time alone. Yet, without preparation, a shield or sword, he killed Goliath with a stone and slingshot. He became the most influential king of Israel and he was a descendant of Jesus. Yet, like any other person, David struggled with self-control. He avoided an upcoming battle to stay home and rest. One evening, he enjoyed some time on the palace's roof when he saw Bathsheba, a married woman, taking a bath. He found out who she was and sent for her. They shared an evening of sexual intimacy and she became pregnant.

Bathsheba's husband Uriah was a soldier in the Israeli army. To cover his and Bathsheba's sin, David called him home from the battle so he would have sex with Bathsheba. An honorable man, Uriah refused to enjoy his wife's bed while other soldiers were on the battlefield.

Disappointed, David did not give up on his need to control the situation so he instructed his general to put Uriah on the frontlines and abandon him, leaving him to die.

After Uriah died, David brought Bathsheba to his home and made her his wife. His emotions of lust and drive for control led him to make a series of horrible mistakes. He eventually repented for his sin and God forgave him, though his and Bathsheba's son died. This series of incidents taught David the importance of self-control and God used him mightily for the nation of Israel. Just as David had to learn, we struggle with applying self-control too and we must think before acting on our emotions because the results could be devastating if we don't

Today's Affirmation:

I will think before I act because it's critical to use self-control in order to live a productive life.

DAY 44: LOVE

Our world has had many historical rifts among various groups. Throughout Biblical history, Jews looked down on the Samaritans and persecuted Christians. During the Holy Crusades, Christians and Muslims fought over religious differences when their stories had so much more in common than they would admit. American settlers stole the land and resources from Native Americans and later built reservations for the remaining Native Americans to live on. Black Americans have been the recipients of racist maltreatment and prejudice since the savage system of American enslavement. The nation divided over the issue of slavery and war broke out, pitting Northern and Southern relatives against one another on the battlefield. South Africans received systematic abuse and mistreatment from their former apartheid government. Because of terrorist attacks by extremists, all Muslims are viewed as terrorists by some people. There are many more examples of racist and prejudicial discord, all of which have no place among people who are called to love one another.

I wish each of us could see one another as individuals rather than as ambassadors of our race, ethnicity or religion. How mightily we could change our world if we were eager to believe the best in others instead of believing ugly stereotypes and assumptions. How wonderful our world would be if people didn't live in fear that they're being judged over racial and ethnic differences. The racial and prejudicial divide our nation and our world continues to grapple with after hundreds of years is ugly, deeply entrenched and heartbreaking. We can't pick and choose which part of it to resolve. ALL of the pieces matter. Love is always eager to believe the best in others. What our world needs now more than anything else is love because every other aspect of happy and healthy relationships flow from love. Each of us must strive to be a better example of love and do our parts to stamp out the hate that divides people who truly need one another to survive.

Today's Affirmation:

I will be an example of love by believing and looking for the best in others and see them as individuals.

DAY 45: JOY

Fathers play a crucial role in the lives of their children. My father was an amazing man. He led, taught by example, loved and disciplined me. Every summer, we had Daddy-daughter week when we had the best adventures together. Daddy taught me how a man should behave as head of the household and he worked diligently to provide. He prayed for me without fail and always had a positive attitude by looking for the best in others. My father was a stellar human being but most of all, the best father I could ever have hoped for. Through I think of and miss him every day since he died, I think more of how blessed I was to be his daughter and I cherish the countless memories built with love.

Once of the main things I learned during grief counseling was to be deliberately and intentionally happy in every moment as a tribute to my father. It helps me intensely because it reminds me during the worst time of my life that there is happiness in every moment, even if it's only a glimmer of joy. Our job is to pay attention to and be grateful for the joyous moments. Another thing that really helped me was thinking about how many people loved my father. There is strength in numbers and no matter where I go, someone has something beautiful to share about my father. That brings me comfort and it strengthens me because it is a joy to know how many people loved him as I did.

Nothing will ever make me feel an ounce of joy that I lost my father's daily presence in my life. What has helped me survive without him is focusing on the years of beautiful memories rather than allowing the pain of losing him dim those wonderful times. There will always be something that hurts us but we have to decide to hold onto our joy. Don't allow anything or anyone to steal your joy. Sometimes holding onto the joyful moments in our lives is the only thing that will help us survive the darkest of times.

Today's Affirmation:

I will be deliberately and intentionally joyful by choosing to find happiness in every moment.

DAY 46: PEACE

So often we chain ourselves to habits. We're rooted to our pasts or sometimes we're conditionally happy if we receive our desired outcomes. We will feel unhappy and anxious about any negative situation until we *decide* to be happy and content. We also have to stop feeling anxious about situations we cannot control. It's up to us to make a conscious change in our mindsct. Otherwise, we will remain attached to and bound by the circumstances and events around it.

It isn't what we go through but how we *grow through* our challenges. It's so critical to maintain a loving heart and to show grace under fire, even when it's the most difficult to do. Being loving and gracious requires a commitment from us on several levels. We have to choose our battles wisely. Some battles are worth the fight whether we win or lose while other battles aren't worth the effort even if we win. When choosing whether to fight, we have to consider our motives and our hearts. It takes two to argue and engage in conflict. Sometimes it's better to walk away from hostile situations and let people argue with themselves instead. Conflict won't steal our joy unless we allow it to. Staying at peace is the ultimate champion's purse.

Another way we can remain at peace is by forgiving those who hurt us. Forgiveness is always the right response, even for those who've hurt us most. Forgiveness doesn't mean we're weak because the ability to forgive makes us strong. Sometimes in order to change our mindsets and reactions, we have to change our habits and let go of the people who wronged us. The changes we make and the release of that pain and grudges frees us from circumstances that would otherwise hold us hostage. Give yourself and others peace with the favor of forgiveness.

Today's Affirmation:

I am at peace. I'm stronger than any habits I have and I'm not a hostage of any negativity.

DAY 47: PATIENCE

When we're waiting and hoping through difficult and trying times that make us feel like our backs are against the wall, the last thing we want to be is patient. One of the most painful experiences we endure is getting past disappointment and pain. A patient attitude is difficult to maintain but it's one of the most critical mindsets we have to have to endure through our challenges.

Each of us has a past. We've all done a thing or two we regret, that's a part of life. It's critical that we learn from our mistakes and keep moving forward. We can't spend our lives hoping and wishing that people won't attack our pasts because so often they will. Being attacked is a painful process that also requires patience. Being betrayed and attacked by someone we considered a friend is a painful experience but those attacks aren't the end of the world. We have to push through with a patient and forgiving attitude. If all they have is our past, they must be challenged by how bright our present and future will be. Wishing doesn't change the past but thinking about it constantly changes our outlook and ability to move forward. Smile. Remain calm and show them love, kindness and grace.

It's difficult to move forward if we dwell on the past and on negative thoughts and feelings. As we wait for things to change, we have to speak about what we want to be and what we want to happen than what could go wrong or about the negativity we're facing. While we're awaiting better days, we have to either release the past and the pain associated with it or live in the past and abandon the future. Sometimes, no matter how desperately we want something, it's more about our attitudes while we're waiting than what we want to happen. Whenever we're stressed or waiting for things to change, we have to be patient. If it hasn't gotten better, then it isn't over. Know that things will change for the better. Believe.

Today's Affirmation:

I will be a patient conqueror by outlasting my disappointments and pain.

DAY 48: KINDNESS

We all make mistakes but what matters most is what we learn, how we react and how we grow as a result. As a recovering perfectionist, I've learned our mistakes aren't millstones around our necks. Our mistakes are teachable moments. We learn to empathize with others rather than judging them. We become better vessels of humility and grace. We learn the monumental power of forgiveness best when we receive it and become more willing to forgive others as a result. Mistakes teach us on an intimate level what it means to grow through adversity. We must use our mistakes as stepping stones and appreciate the grace we receive.

Mistakes are only an installment in our life stories. We cannot close the book on our lives when we make a misstep. We must turn the page, be kind to ourselves and move forward with the benefits of the lessons we've learned and write the next chapter. Just as we turn the page for ourselves, we also need to do the same for others. We can't scoff at others for their mistakes. As difficult as it is when we've been hurt or disappointed, we have to look at everyone as imperfect people who deserve kindness while they're hurting and facing their own challenges.

The relationships we have with other people thrive when we show mercy and love, two prime characteristics of a kind person. We often struggle to forgive others as we speculate on what they've done to us. Yet, God forgives us in spite of His evidence against us. Think of how powerfully kind we could be if we were able to unconditionally forgive, showing the grace and mercy we will inevitably need. I'm eternally grateful for my circle of friends because they've accepted me as I am with all of my imperfections and they forgive me when I make mistakes. Their compassion makes me want to be compassionate toward them and others too.

How can we be powerfully kind today? It will only take a moment but we can change people's lives through the super power of kindness. Let's look for opportunities!

Today's Affirmation:

I will be powerfully kind by forgiving others and showing them the grace and mercy I want when I make mistakes.

DAY 49: GOODNESS

Muhammad Ali is one of the celebrities and world figures I admire most because he had a heart for people. A humble man who was confident in his abilities, he exuded kindness and a rare warmth. As a civil rights activist, he spoke his mind. He had a special gift to love and uplift his race without hating other groups. He made countless public appearances for his fans, especially for children. The all-time best boxer in the world, Ali proved that goodness and kindness aren't weakness but strength and love in action.

Ali was aware of others' needs. When interviewed about his fame and the love others felt for him, he humbly responded that he wished people would love everybody the way they love him. He knew how badly the world and each person in it needs love.

Along with love, Ali lived his life seeking opportunities to be a good person. He was determined to use his fame and the face everyone knew so well to uplift and inspire people all over the world. Wherever he went, he gave of himself freely to others. He never used his fame to take away from people. Instead, he used his celebrity to pour into people with kindness, help and inspiration.

The most beloved and widely acclaimed boxer, Ali also used his words and life to build others up. He never tried to be anyone but himself. He wanted people to know he'd made his share of mistakes along the way but that if he changed even one person's life for good, his life hadn't been in vain. Ali shared a lifetime of motivational jewels and inspiration with the world.

How can we share goodness with the world? Let this be the day we become more caring about others' needs. Look for opportunities to be a ray of goodness to warm the hearts around you and use your life and words to build others up.

Today's Affirmation:

I will be caring and concerned about others. I'll use my words and deeds to build others up.

DAY 50: FAITHFULNESS

We all endure trials and tests but nothing we go through compares to what our mighty God can do when we trust and lean on Him. Speaking positivity during a negative situation isn't denying reality, it's having faith that things will change. Our faith reassures us during moments of fear and doubt that the master plan for our lives surpasses the circumstances of our worst days.

Two biblical characters of great faith come to mind, Esther and Daniel. Esther was faithful to God and her relative Mordecai who reared her once she became an orphan. Esther became a part of the king's harem because of her beauty and charm. Even though most people wouldn't want their daughter to become part of a harem, Mordecai knew it was God's will. Her inner and outer beauty caused the king to choose her as his queen. Eventually, Esther's faith positioned her to stand up for her people, saving the Jews from persecution because of her relationship with the king.

Daniel, a young man of principles who had a deep faith in God and a strong sense of self-control, experienced time in a lion's den. He was thrown in with the lions because he refused to stop worshipping God despite an official government edict that said no one was to worship or pray for thirty days. Daniel survived the lions' den and the king was moved by his faith that led him to worship in spite of his fear of being devoured by the lions.

When we're facing a situation and believe there is no way out or if things aren't working out the way we want them to, we need to ask Him for guidance. We have to believe that God is working on our behalf for what's best for us, not necessarily for what we want. God will meet our impossible needs with His unlimited power. It's our job to believe. It will all work out in the end. If the pieces are still scrambled or missing, it's not the end. Shore up your faith. Believe.

Today's Affirmation:

I will lean on my faith, persevere and never give up because God is faithful to me.

DAY 51: HUMILITY

I've been blessed to live a predominantly fortunate life but it's the most adverse circumstances I've survived over the past fifteen years that have made me a gentler, more humble person. The pain we experience whittles away at our pride and replaces it with compassion for others and a less judgmental attitude. Trying times make us stronger in crucial ways that matter. When harsh experiences make us more compassionate and humble our hearts toward others, we know what it truly means to be strong. Some people think being strong means we never feel or acknowledge pain. The truth is, strong people feel, understand and accept pain and then use the power of their pain to help others.

When we survive and thrive, we realize that other people also experience adversity and that they need love and support far more than they need criticism and contempt. More often than not, the negative things that happen in our lives put us directly on a path to the best experiences and greatest growth we're ever experience. One of the best outcomes is becoming equipped to love someone else through their rough times because we've grown into having a heart for others.

While at a flea market this weekend, I watched a gentleman as he sanded one of the panels on a sideboard he was refurbishing for a customer. He used sandpaper to smooth a few rough patches and, as I watched, I had an epiphany. Just as the sandpaper smoothed the sideboard, our trials and challenges do the same thing for us. Our painful experiences intentionally prepare us to become lighthouses of hope and anchors of love for others when they're going through. Even though hurt people hurt people, we can stop the cycle by taking our pain and using it to better understand and empathize with people. Dare to let your light shine and become a loving example of strength and support for someone who's hurting.

Today's Affirmation:

I will become stronger by learning from the lessons I learn in times of adversity.

DAY 52: SELF-CONTROL

We often strive to control the actions of others and the events around us without exerting as much effort to control ourselves. It's easy to decide what other people should do, especially when we're unaffected by their circumstances and when we don't have to live their consequences. It's even easier to have passionate opinions while observing a situation without the facts. People see our glory or downfalls but rarely know what went on behind the scenes as a backdrop. Instead of talking about another person and what you think they should do or how you think they should behave, stop it. It's not your business. You don't know the entire story and there are at least three sides to every situation. Things are rarely as they seem and that's why we have to use self-control at all times, no matter how difficult it is. We often make the most creative excuses to rationalize where we fall short and why. It's difficult enough to control ourselves so we must accept that trying to control other people is nearly impossible. The choices *we* make today create tomorrow's consequences. Exercising self-control helps us make wise choices.

Self-control is one of the most vital qualities we must cultivate and use in our daily lives. Without self-control, we won't be able to show others patience or kindness if we have a disagreement because our emotions will run unchecked. When we lack self-control, we won't have the ability to do what's best for us and what work for our individual purposes. We have to chart our own course and do what's best for ourselves.

Realize and know that control over *ourselves* is key. Pride and ego prompt us to correct and point out everyone else's flaws while humility guides us to become our best while looking for the best in others. When we're enduring situations where we want to lose our tempers, we can look at them as a workout. Just as our muscles grow from lifting dumbbells and barbells, our self-control broadens when we use it. We have to flex our patience like we do our muscles and stand tall. Will we feed our pride and ego or will we allow humility to develop our self-control?

Today's Affirmation:

I will control my emotions to the best of my ability. I know how important it is for my growth.

DAY 53: LOVE

People define friendship in many ways. I define a friend as someone who knows the good, bad and the ugly about me and loves me anyway. I'm very blessed to have lifelong friends who love me despite my shortcomings and proclivities as well as friends who came into my life later who still love and value me. When thinking of my dearest friends, they love me a lot like the definition of love found in I Corinthians 13. They are patient and kind. When I need a friend they are there for me, even if it isn't my finest hour. They don't insist upon me being who they want me to be, they accept me as I am. When I make a mistake, they forgive and encourage me and they don't hold grudges. Most of all, they've never given up on me or our friendship.

Islam holds friendship in high regard too. The Quran says friends should protect one another. It also says friends are brothers with a responsibility to be merciful and peaceful with one another. The Quran outlines six principles of friendship. Those principles are greeting one another in love, responding when friends need our help and sharing advice among friends. It also includes blessing one another when we're sick and supporting and honoring each other through death.

Judaism recognizes the vital importance of friendship too. Judaism views two as better than one because they can love one another during times of need. Jewish doctrine also, like Christianity and Islam, believes we should love others as we love ourselves, forgive and forgo revenge and be friends to others.

These faiths share universal ideas about friendship. Friendship is so important and pivotal for a happy life. It's how we connect, care for and uphold one another, the way we show love. Be a loving and supportive friend who makes a difference with love.

Today's Affirmation:

I will be a loving friend. My loved ones are wonderful people despite their shortcomings and together we're strong.

DAY 54: JOY

Leprosy is an awful disease that once ravaged people's bodies. It causes joint pain, blisters, skin rashes and ulcers, reduced sensitivity and numbness. The rotting flesh that resulted from leprosy stunk wretchedly. Fingers and toes wasted away, leaving an ugly reminder of leprosy's effects. During biblical times, there was no cure or treatment. Because it was so contagious and its effects were so unsightly, the people forced lepers to live on the fringes of their cities and encampments. If lepers came close to non-lepers, people would yell unclean to warn others. Imaging having a horrid disease that isolates you from loved ones and friends. Leprosy caused physical suffering and emotional and physical alienation.

When Jesus travelled to Jerusalem, he encountered ten lepers. They weren't allowed to come near Jesus so they called out to him for pity and Jesus healed them. When Jesus told them to go to the priests to show they were healed of the dreaded disease, they rejoiced. Of the ten people who Jesus cleansed, only one returned with a joyful, grateful heart and gave praise for cleansing. As a reward for his faith and attitude of gratitude, this leper was not only cleansed but healed and restored.

Being restored was a significant blessing for this lone grateful leper. He become leprosy-free and any limbs or skin he lost when battling the disease regenerated. He was grateful and felt an irreplaceable joy for this unexpected gift. Although he had no idea he would see and meet Jesus that day, the surprise encounter changed his life and he was joyful enough to return to give thanks and express his joy.

Think of a dire situation you faced where you didn't see a victory, yet you emerged victorious. You felt deep joy in that moment and you deserve to feel that kind of joy every day. Find a way to live in joy and to make someone else feel joyful too.

Today's Affirmation:

I will live a joyful life and bring joy into the lives of others.

DAY 55: PEACE

Every day we live, something happens that brings us happiness. The challenge is often that we don't always notice or appreciate the little things because we're anticipating what we yearn for and focused on the outcomes we would prefer. How many times have we surrendered our inner peace because we didn't get what we expected or wanted? Children have a unique ability to feel sheer joy at the smallest things. One of my nephews recently returned home from visiting his grandfather for the summer and was elated to see his room in his family's new home. He was so excited to see his room that I felt joyful because of his joy. He had no grandiose expectations. He lived in the moment and fully appreciated each of the things his parents did for him.

Expectations for the win often block our ability to remember that things have a way of working out to our advantage. We waste so many of our smaller joys living to get what we want that we squander our happiness. We tend to think negatively and before we know it, we articulate them. It's crucial for us to speak life even through our thoughts and we must speak life through our words too. The power of life and death resides in our minds and mouths. Words are so powerfully creative.

As common a cliché as it's become, we must remember not to sweat the small stuff and remain at peace. Just as importantly, we must savor and appreciate even the tiniest joys we're blessed to have. Sometimes the tiniest moments of joy are the times that carry us from one day to the next when we otherwise would lack the motivation to go on. Never surrender the smallest joys in your life because you're waiting on something you see as more significant. Don't squander a single opportunity to feel a moment of joy and don't sacrifice your inner peace to hold out for something bigger. Let today be the day you become determined to hold onto your inner peace and joy by being at peace and choosing to live in the moment.

Today's Affirmation:

I will remain at peace and be content in every situation.

DAY 56: PATIENCE

The past eight years have been my most challenging. My father died unexpectedly from a blood clot after surgery, leaving me devastated with a broken heart. I'd lost my job six years earlier in an extremely unfair, corrupt situation and I've been unable to get gainful employment since then. My home was almost foreclosed. There were days I didn't eat because I couldn't afford groceries and many nights I cried myself to sleep. A relationship with a man I cared for deeply ended two and a half years ago, leaving me alone and unhappy. This man walked away from me soon after my father died, leaving me at a time I needed him most. Other events transpired but those are the major of a series of turbulent experiences.

Yet, from each of these events, some good came. Every pain I've faced has taught me patience. When my father died, I knew nothing would bring him back. The only victory comes from living the kind of life that would make him proud. Joy comes from each memory I have of my times with him. If I hadn't lost my job, I wouldn't have learned how to live in hope while waiting, a critical lesson on patience and faith. When we're unable to wait patiently, we lose the lesson. A love lost left room for the one who genuinely appreciates me to occupy my heart and I'm happier than I've ever been.

Nothing will ever go completely as we want it to all of the time but with the right amount of patience and faith, things will work out in a way that benefits us more than what we could have imagined or asked for. This doesn't mean we should sit back idly and do nothing but it does mean we have to believe things will happen as they should. It takes patience and a willing, open heart to enjoy our lives in tough times. The world didn't give you our peace and it can't take it away. Don't allow anyone or anything to disturb your peace. No matter what you go through, and there will always be something, stay grounded in patience, peace and hope.

Today's Affirmation:

I will be patient and faithful even during my deepest pain.
I believe all things work for my good.

DAY 57: KINDNESS

Kindness is a universal concept across every major religious denomination and tradition. It's a recipe with equal parts of love, compassion and forgiveness. What matters most to improve our world is to show evidence of each of these in our daily lives.

Love, evidenced by kindness, is at its simplest meaning is treating others as we want to be treated. Christians believe in the Golden Rule. The Quran, the Islamic holy text, is even more explicit with the mantra, "Return evil with kindness." Judaism has a similar tenet in the Torah that we are to love our neighbors as ourselves.

Compassion is kindness in action. It's a desire to help others when they're in need. It might be preparing chicken soup for a friend who has a cold or perhaps you could buy groceries for someone who's struggling through unemployment. Giving a friend a kind and nonjudgmental ear after they've made a mistake is also compassionate.

When we love others and have compassion for them, it also becomes easier to forgive. Forgiveness means allowing room when other people make mistakes or have weaknesses. None of us are perfect and forgiveness is a way to love others through grace, acceptance and humility. It helps us to remember that where one of us might be weak in an area, together we are strong. Forgiveness is a way to show others that we value our relationships.

So much of the discord in our world comes from the strife among religions and this strife distracts us from what's most important. What matters most is that we all treat one another with love, compassion and kindness. Today, let's find a way to love other people by showing compassion and kindness. It will make an incredible difference to someone.

Today's Affirmation:

I will treat others well because God loves me in spite of my imperfections.

DAY 58: GOODNESS

We know trees by the fruits they bear. Apple trees yield apples while olives grow on olive trees. Likewise, people are known by the fruits of their labor and actions, a part of their character. Each of us faces challenges and problems that occasionally weigh us down. When we feel pain and angst, what helps us carry on and live fulfilled lives is when we pour into the lives of others. Despite how people treat us, we must behave better toward them and toward others than we've been treated. Making the lives of others better is a firm step toward changing the world with goodness and love. There are times God will use us in someone else's life and we may not see the reason they need us. It might be uncomfortable or something we don't want to do but they need us and we have to follow His will.

All too often, we withdraw from loving others and showing compassion because we've been hurt and have become hardened as a result. When we love in spite of our pain and forgive those who've hurt us, we can make other people's lives happier because we've chosen to become better instead of bitter and weaker. Kindness is never weakness, it's love, strength and humility in action. It takes strength to be resilient enough to make what are often otherwise very difficult choices.

Treat everyone you encounter well because it's the right thing to do. Kindness and compassion open doors money and connections can't always conquer. Our character is who we are and our reputation is what others think we are. What other people think of us and believe about us should have no bearing on how we treat them. Sometimes we have a tendency to give up on people, write them off, and put them in a box of failure. We have to be the person who doesn't give up on anyone. We must remember there is someone who never gave up on us. Let's focus on developing a character of goodness and pour into the lives of others while becoming our best.

Today's Affirmation:

I will treat others well because kindness and goodness are my roots.

DAY 59: FAITHFULNESS

You're an amazing and uniquely gifted person who's destined to achieve amazing things. There is no one like you. The mold broke after your creation and there will never be another you. You're one of a kind and you were born for a unique purpose. You will have setbacks and feel discouraged at times but you cannot give up. Never stop believing in your abilities. Great endeavors take time. The only way you'll sabotage your success is if you quit. Whenever you doubt yourself, have a tough day, pause and have faith in yourself and remember how special you are.

Think of a time in the past when you failed. Reflect on the lessons you learned. You had enough faith to dust yourself off and try again and you will each time you're in a challenging situation because you have faith in yourself. Learn from your past but don't dwell on it. Your future is ahead of you. Look to brighter days with the knowledge you've gained. You will forge forward with the new and build on past lessons. This is the best tactic for a future propelled by faith.

You were born with gifts and talents that are uniquely tailored to your purpose. Your offering to Him is using your gifts and talents to help others and making our world a better place. Remain faithful when facing challenges and setbacks because it will all work out in the end. No matter where you are in life, it you're still breathing, it ain't over. Use every moment to believe, focus, press forward and achieve. NEVER give up on yourself. Nothing and no one can steal your gifts, drain your faith or rob you of your joy. If you're enduring a struggle right now, it might be the lesson you need to move forward. It might not work out the way you thought it would but it will certainly work out the way it should. Keep growing through it and refuse to give up!

Today's Affirmation:

I will overcome every obstacle because I'm an amazing, uniquely gifted person.

DAY 60: HUMILITY

One of the scriptures my father encouraged me to memorize is James 4:10, Humble yourselves in the sight of The Lord, and He shall lift you up. I memorized it but never took it as seriously as I should have until life taught me a powerful lesson about humility. The irony is that we won't know what it truly means to be humble and gracious until we've had the kinds of experiences that build humility within us.

I used to believe humility meant never thinking we are better than others. That's a very significant part of humility but humility also includes thinking of others more often than you think of yourself. Learning to cultivate a spirit of humility is a lot like learning to play a musical instrument. The more a person practices, the better a musician he or she becomes. Just as a musicians develops his or her talent over time, we become more humble and develop a heart for others through experiences and using our humility.

As with most of the gifts that make a monumental difference in our lives, humility is one of the most vital. Without humility, it's difficult to love and be patient with others. It's a challenge to allow our goodness and kindness to shine if we're too prideful. Martez, my friend since childhood, is the epitome of humility. He owns a successful business and whenever he's congratulated for one of his many accomplishments, he always replies that he's still learning and grateful for his success. He is a true entrepreneur who's always willing to help others realize their goals but he is never boastful about anything, though he could boast about his success. He has a kind and loving heart for others and his accomplishments never prevent him from learning. Humility is the path to greatness if we're willing to walk on it and learn. Let each of us cultivate a deeper sense of humility and gratitude for all that we have accomplished and hope to accomplish.

Today's Affirmation:

I will cultivate a deeper sense of humility and remember that what once made me weak will make me stronger.

DAY 61: SELF-CONTROL

Some people can make us angry enough to want to slap them. Think about it. The person delaying traffic back by driving too slowly drives us nuts during rush hour or when we're in a rush. The loud and obnoxious ones who talk and add their own lines during a movie get all sorts of dirty looks. When someone hurts one of our loved ones, we're ready to cuss and fight. As much as we're entitled to our feelings, we still have to hold onto our class and use self-control because we're responsible for our actions and the repercussions that result from what we do.

The Godfather Trilogy is one of my favorite movies because it is full of many valuable life lessons. Santino "Sonny" Corleone is a profound example of why it's necessary to remain calm and think things through calmly and rationally. Sonny died in a brutal bloodbath at a toll plaza because he reacted in so many situations that called for a pragmatist like his younger brother Michael.

It takes a lot of self-control not to respond angrily to people when they hurt us. In a moment of rage and hurt, we want revenge. When we focus on the big payback and having the last word, it clouds our judgment. Responding in anger or rage doesn't make an argument valid, it simply lets the other person know we've lost control. Sometimes we need to take the time to think things though before we respond. There is nothing wrong with waiting until we are able to respond in a calm, rational manner.

Whenever I'm angry and I want to use unkind language with someone, I've learned to meditate on one of my favorite Malcolm X quotes, "A man curses because he doesn't have the words to say what's on his mind." Cursing someone out won't solve the problem and it certainly doesn't help the situation. We can't take our words back once we utter them and hurtful words can cut deeply and ruin relationships. Cooler heads always prevail.

Today's Affirmation:

I will strive to remain in control of my emotions and act instead of reacting.

DAY 62: LOVE

We often grow through situations when we don't understand why we've had to endure sadness and pain. Sometimes God uses our pain to teach us to love other people more deeply. One of the most significant forms of love is showing compassion when others are in pain and getting involved to help people cope when they're hurting and helping to alleviate their pain. There are some things we can only understand if we've experienced them. Pain teaches us the difference between sympathy and empathy. We can easily feel the need to support others but it takes experience to understand and share another person's pain. Both are vital forms of support.

Three of my best friends since childhood were particularly supportive when my father died. They sincerely wanted to support me through the pain and enormity of my loss despite the fact that they'd never experienced the death of a parent. My other two besties have experienced the pain of losing a parent and were also deeply supportive. They cried with me and intimately understood the different stages of grief I would experience. Each of these friends loved me and had the same desire to comfort me through the hurt. The only difference between the love and support shown by these friends, all of which meant the world to me, was sympathetic compassion as opposed to empathetic compassion.

In order to show other people compassionate love, we must broaden our abilities to show others empathy. We have to want to have a compassionate heart for others. We become more understanding about how others feel by putting ourselves in their place when they're hurting, angry or disappointed. This requires us to listen more than we speak. Sometimes listening is one of the most compassionate things we can do and the most appropriate way to show love. We have countless opportunities to show compassion for others and the more often we show compassion, the better we become at loving others.

Today's Affirmation:

I will use the pain I've experienced to love others through their challenges.

DAY 63: JOY

I believe one of the best kept secrets of a happy life is helping others. When we set our minds more on helping others than we do fulfilling our own needs, that's when I believe we get the recipe for the secret sauce of lifelong happiness. John Donne wrote, "No man is an island, Entire of itself." This couplet has been significant to me since my high school English teacher Mr. Mitchem introduced it during a lecture. I've believe we're all connected and we can't live happy lives alone.

During a brief time in my life, I pulled away from everyone, even my family and closest friends. I was depressed and, for the first time in my life, I felt completely hopeless and devoid of joy. I retreated from life, became reclusive and contemplated suicide. I missed countless opportunities to help others, something that used to bring me great joy. My life didn't improve by cutting myself off from people. Instead, life became dark and unhappy. Once I emerged from my funk of self-pity and looked beyond myself, I began having more compassion for people who were going through their own challenges. When I stopped wallowing in self-pity and anger and chose to love and help others again, I began feeling more joy and hope in my life than I had before. I felt like I had a renewed purpose.

The relationship between giving of ourselves to others and increasing our inner happiness seems counterintuitive. Adding happiness to someone else's life takes our minds off of our problems and makes us more optimistic. Enjoy an abundance of happiness in your life by loving and increasing joy among others. Sometimes it's as small as a kind word or compliment to a stranger. It doesn't require a lot of money, time or effort and we don't have to do anything major to bring joy to another person's life. Take advantage of every opportunity to increase joy among others and you will also feel more happiness yourself as a result.

Today's Affirmation:

I will add joy to the lives of everyone around me.

DAY 64: PEACE

How many people are at peace with themselves? Sometimes we're not at peace because we're worried about what others think. We worry we're not enough. Yet, as uniquely created as we are with unduplicated fingerprints and the many talents and gifts we've each been given, we are more than enough.

One of my favorite characters on HBO's *Game of Thrones* is Tyrion Lannister. Born a dwarf, Tyrion's mother died in childbirth. His father resented him, his sister hated him because she believed he killed their mother and his brother pitied him. Tyrion's strengths, among many things, were a heart for others and a fierce intelligence and wit. Despite how the world treated him, Tyrion accepted who he was and lived at peace.

During a conversation with Jon Snow, another favorite character, Tyrion reminded him to acknowledge who he is because no one would ever let him forget it. Tyrion told Jon Snow, "Never forget what you are. The rest of the world will not. Wear it like armor, and it can never be used to hurt you." It was a beautiful scene and I memorized the quote because of how meaningful it is and how it inspires me to be at peace no matter the situation.

As a dwarf, Tyrion advised Jon Snow well because Jon is constantly reminded that he is an illegitimate son.

No matter what anyone says to you or about you behind your back, never forget how unique you and blessed you are. No one is perfect and growth is a lifetime process. It is so important to be at peace about who we are and accept who we are as we continue to grow and improve. Remember that no one can be a better you than you can and that you're not obligated to live to any person's standards for your life. Remain at peace and believe that you are enough just as you are and that you have the ability within you to become all you're destined to be.

Today's Affirmation:

I will remain at peace with myself. I am enough and powerful because I will become all I am purposed to be.

DAY 65: PATIENCE

One of the worst times to make a decision is when we're angry, afraid or impatient. Each of these emotions can cause us to make impulsive decisions we would not otherwise make and they also make us reactionary. Whatever controls our minds controls us. Anger drains our patience, kills our joy and robs us of hope. Fear makes us dwell on the worst things that could happen instead of the positive things we hope for. Impatience makes us rash and prevents us from thinking as clearly as we should. Our worst times, no matter how horrid, won't last forever. We must be patient in order to avoid the pitfalls of anger and impatience.

Walt Disney heard the answer "No" 302 times before he was able to secure funding to open The Magic Kingdom at Disney World. If he'd become bitter and decided to throw in the towel after hundreds of rejections, over 25 million people wouldn't have visited Disney World each year and Disneyland, Tokyo Disney, Euro Disney and several other amusement parks that are a part of the Disney empire.

Dwayne The Rock Johnson is another celebrity who struggled before getting his biggest break. After his dream to become a professional football player with the NFL ended, he played professional football briefly for the Canadian Football League. When he was cut from the team's roster, Johnson became depressed and angry. Once he was cut from the football team, he entered professional wrestling. From there, he's had a sizzling film and television career. He even found time to share his story with the world by writing an autobiography. What if The Rock had given up? We wouldn't enjoy multiple films and the HBO television sensation *Ballers* and we would never be inspired by how he's overcome so many obstacles.

    No matter what happens, never give up. Be patient and believe that things will work out for the best because they will as long as you don't give up.

Today's Affirmation:

I will be patient enough not to make decisions in anger, fear or impatience.

DAY 66: KINDNESS

During a recent hair appointment, I read a few magazines and learned about several heartwarming celebrity acts of kindness. As a hip hop and rap music fan, I was delighted to learn how Drake and The Game helped an Ohio woman whose boyfriend and children died in a house fire by paying the funeral expenses. I also discovered The Game's Robin Hood Project, an initiative he started to donate a million dollars to people who needed help.

T.I., a Southern hip hop artist, restaurateur and television and movie producer and star, has saved two lives. When I read *Sinner's Creed*, Scott Stapp's book, I discovered that T.I. found Stapp after he'd fallen from a hotel balcony after overindulging in alcohol and drugs. T.I. made sure Stapp received emergency care and undoubtedly saved his life. T.I. also prevented another man from committing suicide. He told the man in a personal message that his life was too precious to commit suicide and he waited to talk to him personally once police were able to get him to leave the roof where he had threatened to jump and end his life.

Denzel and Pauletta Washington are also known for their kindness. Omari Hardwick, heartthrob of Starz powerhouse *Power*, coached and substitute taught their oldest son John. Hardwick has spoken openly about how the Washingtons helped him while he was a struggling, homeless actor. He was discouraged and when he was about to lose his car to repossession, the Washingtons paid the fees and Hardwick was able to keep his car. Hardwick's genuine kindness toward and interest in the Washington's son opened the door for him to establish a relationship with the Washingtons that changed his life when he needed help most.

It's easy to allow negative events to harden our hearts. The daily challenges we face remind us how important it is to be kind to others and to share what we have with others without hesitating. Being able to give and pour into others is kindness in action. Although all of us can't afford to give as much money as celebrities often give, we can seize every opportunity to show kindness to others and help them in ordinary ways that are equally as meaningful.

Today's Affirmation:

I will show kindness at every opportunity presented to me because no act of kindness is too small.

DAY 67: GOODNESS

The racial divide our nation continues to grapple with after hundreds of years is ugly, deeply entrenched and heartbreaking. We can't pick and choose which part of it to resolve because ALL of the pieces matter. Unfortunately, many of the stakeholders in each group are vested solely in how they feel and what they believe rather than in working collaboratively to close the racial divide. We must remember that when we disagree with someone else's ideas, it doesn't diminish their feelings or opinions. Making assumptions and jumping to conclusions never helps us understand others or their opinions. We can make assumptions about why hurting people do the things they do but we will never know their pain if they don't articulate it to us. We can't draw conclusions, we must be a listening ear because that's the only way we will ever come to an understanding.

The events that unfolded during the summer of 2016 are unspeakably horrific. Yet, several good things have come of them. People have united in grief and are talking to one another about their feelings and even listening to one another's differences. Second, the senseless deaths of innocent men murdered by police and the police officers who were injured and murdered in retaliation and anger have become catalysts for peace and change Americans can believe in and build on.

Undeniably, everything happens for a reason. How we choose to deal with our challenges matters because our response defines us. The way our national and state leaders deal with these senseless tragedies defines them. May God bless each of us as we move forward. Let goodness stand out, making otherwise senseless injuries and deaths stand for peace, unity and healing.

Today's Affirmation:

I will look for goodness in others because I value unity, peace and healing.

DAY 68: FAITHFULNESS

No matter what faith we practice, prayer is an important part of it. No faith is superior to another and there is value in every faith. As a Christian, I believe in God and the power of prayer. Prayer gives us strength and grace under pressure. Prayer comforts us when we are hurting and it helps us comfort others when they're in pain. We pray to be equipped to handle all that comes our way because no matter what happens, God sees it, He feels it and He will address our needs in His time when we need Him most.

Each of us has faced and will face adversity. All things work for our good when we're able to learn from our challenges and use the pain we experience to grow and help others grow. We are never what happens to us when we remember and realize that things happen for us rather than to us. We are the sum total of our choices as we rise and move forward.

Prayer is a process where we ask for the desires of our hearts and God gives us three answers – yes, no and not right now. Max Lucado wrote in his book *He Still Moves Stones* that "Faith is not the belief that God will do what you want. It is the belief that God will do what is right." I added this quote to my vision board because it reminds me daily how important faith is and how much we grow when we're faithful and living in faith. We grow most during the periods of no and not right now. When we don't get the desires of our hears, we have to consider that perhaps God has delayed or denied our prayers because He wants to increase our faith or give us something better than we've hoped for.

Consider how important it is to increase our faith. It's time to cast all of our cares. We can pray and release our cares or we can cling to them and worry but we cannot do both. We must believe and make faith our pillow.

Today's Affirmation:

I will remain faithful at all times. With God, I am equipped to handle anything that comes my way.

DAY 69: HUMILITY

People will gossip about us. There's no way around it and there's no way to escape it. There is a way, however, to handle it peacefully and with class. First, we must remain humble. We can't worry or become anxious because some people don't like us. We're not living for approval and so many people don't even love themselves so they have a difficult time loving others.

People who make ugly, snide and inaccurate comments about others destroy their own reputations and happiness. They spew poison that contaminates their spirits. We can't satisfy the need to defend ourselves in indefensible situations by allowing pride to put us on the warpath to engage with bitter people. Some battles aren't worth fighting, even when we're right because when people are committed to disrespecting or misunderstanding us, they won't listen to reason.

One of the most difficult things to do sometimes is to give others the grace and mercy we want when they've hurt and disappointed us. Too often we retaliate when people make a mistake instead of showing love and forgiveness. We can't let another's misstep poison our spirits. Showing love and forgiveness when we're hurt isn't easy but it isn't impossible. The greatest stride we can make in our lives is a step toward living with greater love and humility for others. People will hate us, low rate us, dog us out and leave us for dead. We have to remember that God sees, He hears and He will make them our footstools. One of the most cathartic things we can do is recognize where we are our own worst enemy and make peace.

It hurts to be gossiped about and mistreated. When we or someone we love endures such situations, we have to remember we're being forged in the fire and that we have to keep moving forward. We'll each rise as a phoenix, better, stronger and changed. Keep on keeping on!

Today's Affirmation:

I will forgive and show others the grace and mercy I want, even if I don't believe they deserve it.

DAY 70: SELF-CONTROL

Things will always happen that are beyond our control and we can't allow these things to change who we are or how we react. Each day, we have the luxury of deciding what kind of attitude we want to embrace and how we will face our challenges. It's up to us to control our attitudes and responses. One thing we can choose to do is maintain a positive attitude.

Self-control requires an enormous amount of discipline and determination. Allowing negativity to seep into our minds and relationships with others is dangerous and toxic. It eats at us, claws at us and draws us into things we shouldn't be a part of. We must set our minds and decide to look for the light in situations. One of the most valuable lessons we can learn is how to master control of ourselves and our actions. Until we do, we will struggle as we deal with the events and surprises the day brings. Life is unpredictable and it won't adjust to us so we must make the adjustments. We can choose to either be weighed down by the foolishness that hurts and irritates us or we can release it and enjoy our lives. It isn't always an easy choice but we must choose what's best for us.

Decide today to take a firm control over your agenda and emotions so you are at the helm of all you do.

You will have distractions but you can manage them as long as you manage your emotions. Uncontrolled emotions can ruin relationships, reputations and our general happiness. Don't allow anything or anyone to keep you from accomplishing your daily goals. Emotions are changeable and variable, not a sufficient foundation on which we can build our lives. As humans, we have feelings and the way we feel is very important. We have to be steady, unchanging and aware of our feelings and how they will affect us. Never deny your emotions but don't allow them to run unchecked either.

Today's Affirmation:

I will remain conscious of my emotions and how they can affect me. I will do my best to manage my reactions to situations.

DAY 71: LOVE

We talk often about loving others, our possessions and so many other things but not nearly often enough about how much we love our lives. We have to learn to embrace life. Life will never be the way we always want it to be but we must be grateful to be alive. Bruce Lee once said, "If you love life, don't waste time, for time is what life is made of." He was right. Every day is a brand new opportunity for fresh start and we'll only win with positive attitudes. Loving our lives requires us to stop promoting the negatives and begin emphasizing the positives. Life is what we make it and it's up to us to find reasons to be grateful, joyful and alive.

Our lives won't always be joyful but we can set our minds to look for joy in all things and live with enthusiasm by taking charge of our lives. That means we have to chart our own courses and fulfill our individual purposes no matter what anyone else has to say. Every step we take toward fulfilling our purpose matters. We won't always have everything we want and that's often a good thing. Sometimes the things we want aren't best for us and we can only be grateful for the outcomes we received. Often, the less we need and demand, the more we attract.

Just as we want to be accepted by others and make our own decisions, it's easier to fall in love with our own lives when we respect the will of others. Too often we squander our joy by trying to force other people to do what we want them to do or what we believe is best for them. They will continue to act as they feel is best for them whether we agree or not. No matter how we feel about someone else's decisions or actions, we cannot overstep our bounds and we can't lose any of our peace.

Make a conscious decision to LIVE instead of merely existing. Fall in love with your life. A bounty of wonderful experiences await the opportunity to inspire you and bring you joy.

Today's Affirmation:

I will love and embrace every moment of my life and appreciate every day I'm blessed to live.

DAY 72: JOY

People don't steal our peace or joy, we surrender it to them. Each of us is the commander in chief of our own peace and joy and we must never surrender either to anyone. If anyone had an excuse to dwell in misery and drown in self-pity, Tyler Perry did. He grew up on the streets of New Orleans and lived in an abusive household. Since childhood, he struggled and sacrificed to make his dreams come true. Encouraging himself, Perry experienced an existential wakeup call by writing himself letters that forced him to think about who he was and what he wanted. He invested his life savings in making his dreams come true with performances of a musical he wrote and failed when no one came to see the performances. Not one to give up, he kept pushing forward despite sleeping many nights in motels and his car. Today, Tyler Perry owns his own studio and is a force to be reckoned with in television, film and stage plays.

Callan Mulvey, a dashing actor from New Zealand who portrays the villain Milan on the engaging Starz series *Power*, was in a horrific head on collision. An actor's nightmare, his face sustained significant damage. He endured reconstructive surgery where his face and jaw were repaired with multiple titanium plates. Mulvey also sustained injuries to his knee and ankle. He didn't give up his dream of performing on television or movie screens. He held onto the joy of performing and has become an international star, starring in motion pictures like *300: Rise of an Empire* and *Captain America: The Winter Soldier*. Had he given up during his reconstructive surgeries, we wouldn't know how talented he is.

It's easy to think of our misery and our problems but it's also very harmful. When we dwell on our challenges, we leave little time to exercise our faith in God and our hope. Just as our words are powerful, so are our thoughts. No matter what happens in our lives, there is always something beautiful to feel joyful about. We aren't able to think this way until we change our mindsets. When we think of our lives, we have to focus on the beautiful and joyous parts. We have to believe in our futures and become prisoners of hope. By doing so, our joy will increase.

Today's Affirmation:

I will focus on living a joyful future because my past has no bearing on my future.

DAY 73: PEACE

An attitude of gratitude helps us maintain a happy, peaceful life. How often do we take what we have for granted by thinking more about what we don't have? Our lives thrive according to what we prioritize. If we feed positivity, it will multiply in our lives but if we feed negativity, it will destroy our inner peace and joy. That's why we must carefully and deliberately choose what we dwell on. We would be much happier if we thought more about what we love than what we don't like because positive, grateful thoughts are the foundation of an attitude of contentment.

There are benefits to having an attitude of contentment. Contentment brings us inner peace and that reduces our stress levels, increases the positivity with which we view the world and it makes our lives so much more enjoyable. Content people focus on the blessings and happiness they have, not what they *don't* have. It's a magnet for happiness. When we are grateful for what we have, we magnify our happiness. When we take our blessings for granted and dwell more on what we don't have, we create emotional voids in our lives and try to use material possessions and other trappings to fill them. The less we need, the more we attract.

An attitude of contentment leads us to a lifestyle that blesses us even more abundantly. Our struggles are real, there's no doubt about that. Our blessings are real and there's no doubt about that either. It's up to us to decide which is most important to focus on. When we invest in helping others, we feel a joy we wouldn't have from helping ourselves and it makes us appreciate what we have even more. Our blessings aren't just for us. We are blessed to BE a blessing.

Contentment brings greater peace into our lives and it helps us continue to grow. With a peaceful and grateful heart, be content but don't ever become complacent.

Today's Affirmation:

I will be peaceful, content and grateful for all of my blessings while working hard to evolve.

DAY 74: PATIENCE

One of the most difficult qualities to develop is patience but its benefits are often beyond our wildest expectations. Patience is powerful and it makes it possible for us to hold on to our hope and joy in difficult times. Patience keeps our egos in check. We realize everything isn't about us. Instead of giving up when a situation doesn't change us as quickly as we expect it to, we learn that we have to be willing to press on, live our lives and learn the lessons that are folded into the pain and delays.

If we keep in mind that our setbacks and challenges are stepping stones to better, sweeter days, we will become more successful than we ever hoped to be. Steve Jobs and Steve Wozniak refused to give up on their dreams. They invested their time and a lot of patience. Jobs sold his car and Wozniak sold his calculator so they could afford to create a model of the computer we know as the Apple I. What if they'd given up? There would be no iPhones, no iMacbooks, no iTunes and no Apple Watch.

Dreams don't come true on our timetable and sometimes they are fulfilled very differently from what we anticipated. Two of the most difficult things we experience are waiting for our dreams to be fulfilled and accepting what happens when we don't get the outcome we wanted.

That's when we have to be open to being where we are and content. No experiences we have are wasted, especially when we must wait, because we learn and become more faithful and stronger. The longer the process, the more we appreciate a victorious outcome. We have to forget what lies behind us, maintain an attitude of perseverance and press on. The patience we develop during our challenging times helps us to lead happier, more content and productive lives. Dream new dreams! Be patient. Believe.

Today's Affirmation:

I will meet my goals and I won't give up during times I have to wait. I will be content even when things don't go the way I expected them to.

DAY 75: KINDNESS

India Arie collaborated with Sergio Mendes on a wonderful song called "Timeless." My favorite lines from the song have become my mantra. Those lines, "Kindness is timeless, love is so easy to give, It just takes a moment to show somebody that you care," are so true. Imagine how much happier our society would be if we all felt and lived this way. Kindness really is timeless and it never goes out of style. It is very easy, almost effortless, to be kind. A smile, saying hello or holding the door for a stranger is kindness in action are all easy ways to show consideration and compassion.

We live in a stressful world with so many distractions. We're so often preoccupied with looking at our phones, rushing through conversations to get our points across and complaining about all of the many things we have to do. In truth, all of us are busy but that doesn't mean we don't have the time to show kindness and courtesy to others. Just as often as we carry silent burdens, we have no idea what those around us are going through. The moment we spend encouraging someone else could make a significant difference in their lives and it will make us feel good to make someone else smile.

That's why it's so important to be a little kinder than necessary. The best part of taking a few seconds to increase someone else's happiness is that it doesn't cost a thing, we don't have to exert much of an effort and it also increases our own joy. Compliment someone sincerely. Encourage them if they're depressed or struggling with a challenge. Bite your tongue if someone insults you instead of firing off an angry response. Each of us is here to make a difference. Whatever acts of kindness you choose, do it from your heart and touch the heart of another.

Today's Affirmation:

I will be available to others. It's important for me to be kinder than necessary.

DAY 76: GOODNESS

As a child, I loved superheroes, especially Superman. I believed we had a lot in common because he was adopted like me. Known commonly as Clark Kent, he was an orphan who a Kansas family adopted and reared with strong, traditional values, among them trust, love and kindness, all of which developed a goodness in Superman. Though he was a superhero, the way he was reared heavily contributed to his determination to use his powers for the good of mankind.

Superman chose to use his powers for good to help others and was modest enough to do so behind a hidden identity at the recommendation of his father. How many of us could have superpowers and not want to flex them just a little? Could we help others selflessly without recognition and acclaim? Would we want to be worshipped as the superhero?

As an iconic superhero, Superman inspired us. He seemed invincible. Yet, even he had a weakness, kryptonite. Kryptonite weakened Superman dramatically because it diminishes his powers. Too much kryptonite could kill him. Even superman, every child's hero, had a weakness. Yet, he dedicated his life to uplifting people, taking care of others' needs and seeking opportunities to show goodness to others.

Superman is a fictitious hero but his desire to help others and fight for justice and fairness is a genuine and admirable quality of goodness we should all emulate. Today, find someone you can be a superhero to and serve them. It won't cost anything but time and effort. When people need help you can become a superhero in moments without dashing into a phone booth to change into a costume, cape and mask. You don't need to leap tall buildings or fly. Dare to take the challenge to use your super power of goodness.

Today's Affirmation:

I will be a superhero for those who need my help and accept my mission to uplift others.

DAY 77: FAITHFULNESS

I believe God blesses us to be a blessing to others. We used to sing a song in church about how we can't beat God giving. One of the lines that stands out to me most is, "The more you give, the more He gives to you." I didn't understand its significance as a child but I certainly do now. We are blessed to be a blessing and when we're faithful to God by helping others, He remains faithful to us.

Steve Harvey is one of my favorite media personalities and philanthropists. He has had multiple hosting jobs and starred in several television shows and movies. Steve is a published author and his book *Act Like A Lady, Think Like A Man* is the basis for two very successful films. Not only is he unabashedly honest about his experiences, his past and some mistakes he's made, but he also uses his blessings to help others.

Steve's life hasn't always been easy . During the late eighties, he was homeless and sleeping in his car when he performed comedy shows that did not include a hotel in his contracts. He showered at gas stations or public bathrooms. Many people forget their past once they become successful but Steve remains faithful to helping others. From what I've seen in articles and heard in various interviews, Steve understands the concept of giving quite well. Steve and his beautiful wife Marjorie founded and operate The Steve and Marjorie Harvey Foundation, to provide outreach for fatherless children through education, mentoring and worldwide programs that help children become leaders. His radio and talk show honors people who are making a difference and both shows reach out to help people in need. That's being faithful to the God who blessed you and being faithful to other people by helping them when they're in need.

It doesn't require a fortune like Steve's to help others, only a willing, loving heart. Let this be the day we decide to be faithful in helping others too.

Today's Affirmation:

I will help others and be a blessing to them. I'm faithful because I realize my blessings are not just for me.

DAY 79: HUMILITY

We all make mistakes and we should never be ashamed of this reality. Our mistakes confirm our humanity and capacity for self-development and growth. We will make mistakes until the day we die. That's why it's imperative for us to love ourselves and be gentle while we're learning valuable lessons from our mistakes. Having a spirit of humility doesn't mean we think lowly of ourselves. It means we think of others and their needs more often than we think of ourselves.

Our mistakes are stepping stones to stronger, kinder and move loving selves. Sometimes we allow our mistakes to stunt our growth and hold us back. We begin to pity ourselves. Self-pity causes us to focus inward, a destructive form of pride. When we put ourselves down, it's not in love and our self-pity makes us more susceptible to other people walking all over us. When other people put us down while we're wallowing in self-pity, we sometimes become paralyzed by fear or negativity and we're ready to give up. We can't be so overcome by our thoughts and that we fail to act and press forward.

Every mistake will either make us weaker or stronger. The beautiful thing is it's our choice which it will be. We can either wallow in disappointment or choose responsibly by standing tall and working hard. Forgiving ourselves is a necessity. That's why we have to use our mistakes as opportunities to grow, improve and to help others along the way when they make mistakes. Someone will always try to bring us down. That doesn't mean we have to further the agenda by being ashamed of anything. When people remind us of our mistakes, we have to hold our heads high and know in our hearts that we are forgiven and, most importantly, we have to release the pain and focus on the lessons.

Today's Affirmation:

I will not be ashamed of my mistakes because they are stepping stones to a better me.

DAY 80: SELF-CONTROL

We have emotions and we are meant to experience them. Anger is a human emotion and it's normal to become angry at times. Even Jesus became angry while dealing with moneylenders and merchants when he began flipping tables and drove them out of the temple. Our emotional responses only become a problem when we allow them to control us. Out of control anger can cause an avalanche of problems we weren't looking for. Living a stressful life with challenges we must face is a reality we can't escape. What we can manage is to refuse to allow other people to pull us into their anger and unhappiness. Of course that's easier said than done without having coping skills. We must make every effort not to respond in anger when people angrily confront us. Their anger should not become our problem. It takes a lot of self-control to remain at peace with others and it's always worth the effort.

With helpful coping mechanisms, we can control our impulses to react to volatile, chaotic situations. Staying angry consumes so much of our energy unnecessarily. We cannot avoid our anger. We have to acknowledge and deal with it. When we hold onto anger, it can make us physically ill, passively aggressively angry at people who haven't done anything to us and our anger seeps over into and taints our relationships with our loved ones. It's also important to find more positive ways to channel our anger once we acknowledge it. Some people count to ten while others remove themselves from the company of others long enough to calm down before reacting. Exercise and meditation are other helpful means of dealing with anger too.

It's crucial for us to hold onto the key to our happiness. We can't allow negative events to control our actions and reactions because anger is a fleeting emotion we must control before it controls us.

Today's Affirmation:

I will not allow anyone to pull me out of my peace and into their chaos.

DAY 81: LOVE

Oscar Wilde once said, "To love oneself is the beginning of a lifelong romance." This is a tried and true statement. A healthy love for self is the foundation for all we do and it helps us love others. So often, I hear people say we can't love anyone else until we learn to love ourselves, so much so that it's become a trite expression despite how true it is. Yet, so many of us don't love ourselves and it's evident in how we treat ourselves and others.

A humble love for ourselves helps us love others. Our lives become happier and healthier when we make better choices about what we do and how we spend our time. Healthy self-love helps us realize how critical it is to take care of ourselves in order to care for others. How many times do we help others put on their proverbial oxygen masks when we're not even wearing our own? Self-love also makes us independent. Independence helps us become truer to ourselves and who we're purposed to be. Once we achieve our purpose, we blossom and begin using our gifts to help and uplift others. To function at our highest level and help others is a high form of self-love.

Self-love enables us to set healthy boundaries. We put up with less foolishness and become firm about what we should and should not do. We also stop being dependent on acceptance and approval from the outside. We flourish as independent, strong people. Ultimately, each of these forms of self-love helps us love others without hurting ourselves. It's impossible to love people if we're empty ourselves. We can only give others the love we give ourselves.

It's important for us to love and appreciate ourselves, flaws and all. We have to embrace ourselves no matter what happens. Let this be the day we begin to love ourselves without reservation.

Today's Affirmation:

I will love myself in a healthy manner and always remember I'm precious and valuable.

DAY 82: JOY

There are far too many Debbie Downers in our world who enjoy spreading negativity. They thrive on being haters and will share their daggers of pessimism with anyone who will listen. No one can deny that we live in a challenged world with sad moments but the sad moments offer the unique opportunity to uplift others. Our struggles are real but so are our blessings. It's up to us to decide what's most important to focus on. We've all faced dismal challenges and we're still here with a 100% survival rate. What if more of us decided to take Ralph Waldo Emerson's advice and scattered joy?

Ellen DeGeneres is a genius when it comes to scattering joy through her daily show. Each time I watch The Ellen DeGeneres Show, I'm happier and much more optimistic. One of my favorite Ellen show segments is the interview with Demarjay Smith, the inspirational, aspiring eight year old Jamaican personal trainer who has become famous through his workout videos. After a brief interview, Ellen surprised Demarjay with a surprise introduction to Olympian Usain Bolt. It was incredible to see the joy in his eyes when he met Bolt, received a basket of gifts and the thrill he felt when he had the opportunity to race Bolt. Those are moments of joy Demarjay will never forget and the segment brought joy to viewers and the studio audience too.

Scattering joy takes minimal effort. We don't need an international platform like Ellen's to inspire a child or motivate our family and friends, celebrate their accomplishments or congratulate them . We can spread joy with a smile, hug or genuine compliment. We can scatter happiness by speaking life over negative situations. A simple word of encouragement plants hope and leads to joy. We would radically change our world by scattering joy. Positivity is contagious once we make it a lifestyle. Decide to scatter joy. Not only will you make others happy but you'll become happier too.

Today's Affirmation:

I will scatter joy everywhere I go!

DAY 83: PEACE

It's difficult to remain at peace when we're worried about our challenges and even more difficult when we're preoccupied with things beyond our control. It's normal to be concerned about finding a job when you're unemployed. It's normal to think about the possibility of foreclosure and interrupted utilities when we unable to meet our financial obligations. Divorce causes a lot of pain and unhappiness and so does wanting to be in a quality relationship when we're alone. With these and so many other stressors that we could unexpectedly face, it's important to find a way to maintain inner peace and calmness.

One way to maintain our inner peace is appreciating what we have instead of focusing on what we lack. If we stopped complaining and started being grateful, our lives would immediately improve and so would the lives of the people we complain to. Gratitude boosts our joy and ability to focus on what we need to do in order to move forward in difficult times. With gratitude and a future forward focus, we can avoid being preoccupied with what we can't do and we won't fear the unknown.

We must learn to rest and withdraw from stressful activities and people. We can either be weighed down by people who hurt us or we can release them with love and enjoy our lives. Our calendars don't drive our lives. We plan or say yes to the events on our calendars. We must stop overextending ourselves and then complaining about choices we made.

Inner peace also comes when we allow people to be who they are without trying to mold them into what we believe they should be. Each of us is uniquely gifted and we bring special qualities to the world. No one has to be less of who they are to be accepted. Give people the room to be themselves. We have to stop wanting others to change and appreciate them for who they are.

Let this be the day you begin to embrace inner peace. Do what's best for you and remember that many wonderful experiences await the opportunity to inspire and bring you joy. The more positive your thoughts and posts are, the more positive your life will become. Thoughts and words are powerfully creative. Choose carefully and wisely so you can live in peace.

Today's Affirmation:

I will strive to maintain inner peace at all times. I live my best life when I'm at peace.

DAY 84: PATIENCE

My mother often tells me, "Fools rush in where angels fear to tread." It took years for me to understand exactly what she meant. Sometimes, no matter how urgently we feel about a situation, we need to stop and think before speaking and making any decisions or moves. Sometimes rushing into things is worse than dragging our feet. We often have to be patient and stay the course when we're developing an idea or working on a project. It could take longer than we anticipated while launching our ideas to attain the level of success we want. What's most important is that we don't give up.

It's also important to be patient with other people no matter how difficult they become to deal with. We have a tendency to give up on people in exasperation, write them off and put them in a box of failure. We have to learn to be the person who doesn't give up on anyone. We have to remember that there is someone who never gave up on us. Miracles really do happen every day and we have to be willing to be a part of the miracle.

Milton Hershey's life is a prime example of patience and resilience. After leaving school in the fourth grade, he had several jobs until his mother arranged his apprenticeship to learn to make candy. Milton Hershey started three candy companies and each of them failed. It wasn't until he began his fourth company, Hershey, that he became a success and a giant in the candy industry. I'm sure there were times Hershey wanted to give up but he didn't. Today, as a testimony to his resilience, we enjoy Hershey's Kisses, Reese's Peanut Butter Cups and a host of other delicious candies. Hershey Park in Pennsylvania is also a part of Hersey's legacy.

      Whenever you're tempted to give up on yourself or someone else, think of a time where patience prevailed. Don't allow anyone to make you shrink or feel inadequate. You're wondrously made and there are marvelous, unique things about you. Everyone you meet will not understand you or your purpose. Set your mind on your goals. Run and complete your race and refuse to allow anyone or anything hold you back. Nothing of value comes easily and nothing is accomplished when we give up. Be patient, resilient and never ever give up!

Today's Affirmation:

I will be patient with myself and others. Patience and resilience are essential!

DAY 85: KINDNESS

The relationships that cause the deepest pain often teach us the most about forgiveness and compassion. We learn the most about how to treat others when we've been mistreated. Pain will come into our lives and it's sometimes not a result of anything we've done or "asked for." The gift in these situations is the lesson we learn through the experience and the resulting depths of kindness and compassion we develop.

I learned so much about forgiveness and compassion through my divorce. Adjusting to marriage as a newlywed is often challenging. My ex husband sprung an executive decision I didn't agree with on me without asking my opinion or considering my feelings. At the time, it was far more important than it would be now. He went through with his decision and it affected our marriage very negatively. The divide between us grew. Eventually, when I was ready to forgive and work on improving our marriage, he'd developed a relationship with another woman. When she became pregnant, he divorced me to marry her.

At the onset, I was devastated. What spouse wouldn't be? Infidelity is painful and humiliating and the birth of an outside child is an entirely different level of betrayal. This experience made me extremely bitter and angry for a long time. Yet, as hurtful and degrading as this betrayal was, it became a poignant reminder of how important it is to forgive quickly and to have compassion for those who hurt me the most. It was also a vivid reminder of how important it is to be everything you want to receive in a relationship.

Our imperfect relationships can be catalysts that prepare us to be better friends, partners and spouses in the future. It doesn't matter if we believe someone deserves to be forgiven. We should forgive them because we deserve the peace and joy that come with releasing them from our debt. The power of forgiveness has an amazing transformational power. Reflect on how your relationships have made you kinder, more compassionate and more loving. Never allow anyone or any experience to make you bitter and steal your joy and kindness.

Today's Affirmation:

I will be kinder and stronger because the pain I've experienced teaches me how it feels to be hurt. My pain equips me to be compassionate with other people.

DAY 86: GOODNESS

Encourage others and uplift their spirits at every opportunity. Our world has far too many freelance critics and not nearly enough professional encouragers. We don't have to be perfect, pious or overly religious to remind people that goodness and love exist in our world. Having character doesn't mean we don't make mistakes. It means we face the consequences of our mistakes while believing all things work for our good. That's *character*!

God always reveals things and people at the best time for us. It's our responsibility to listen and act accordingly. When we look at others, we must do so with an open mind and kind, gentle heart. So many people feel unaccepted and unloved. It's up to each of us to spread love. When someone hurts us, it's normal to become angry and hurt and even to want revenge. The worst thing we can do is become who hurt us and then hurt others. One thing I imagine we all want to experience from others is compassion and forgiveness.

Our heart's true state of being is reflected in our thoughts and the way we treat others. Over the past decade, I've had the opportunity to see how very blessed I am to have friends in my life who love me at my best and worst. They remained by my side when I wasn't my most lovable, comforted me through some of the most horrible times in my life and never gave up on me. That's goodness and love in action. Their unending love and encouragement inspired me to enjoy life again and to stop mourning what was and walk into my new purpose.

Our connections matter in every aspect of your life. If we're connected to takers, we'll give without being replenished. If we're connected to loving people, love will flow in your lives. People who need and are faithful to other people are the happiest in the world. That's why we have to maintain healthy, happy and whole connections.

Be the best friend you can for those you love. Be the person who helps others believe and have hope again, who rekindles joy among those you love and add to their vibrant lives. The amount of kindness, love and honesty you give determines the level of each you'll attract. You might not believe it but the way you treat others matters. Be an example of goodness!

Today's Affirmation:

I will be an encourager. I'll look for opportunities to uplift others.

DAY 87: FAITHFULNESS

About seven or eight years ago, I came across a quote that changed my spiritual outlook and level of faith. This quote by St. Augustine, "God loves each of us as if there was only one of us," caused me to meditate on a personal level for the first time about the immeasurable depth and width of God's love for and faithfulness to us. I was enduring some very difficult circumstances that roused greater faith and hope they roused within me at the time I needed it most.

The quote spoke to me in several other ways too. As I reflected on how essential my faith had become to me, it reminded me to strive to be as faithful to God as I could be. It also reminded me to be as faithful to others as I can, especially when they're facing difficult times. That's when people need our love most, just as we need God's love. It reinforced the fact that we should never assume someone doesn't know God based on our judgment of them. We can't see the good He so faithfully sees. What we interpret as negativity could be caused by the pain or unhappiness of the very circumstances God is using to do a powerful work in them.

This quote also encouraged me to show others the most powerful and faithful love I can. Rather than looking for lesser qualities in others, pointing out faults or being highly critical, I learned to mine for gold in others. Everyone has golden points and it's up to us to emphasize their best qualities because it shows our faith to see the good in others and we're showing love in action. When we are in a faithful relationship with Him, He enhances our other relationships in ways we never imagined possible. It's His love in us and faithfulness to us that gives us the capacity to love others and ourselves.

      Love others enduringly. Let your love be faithful and continuous. Let it be of such depth and width that it has no bounds. That's faith in Him we can put into action for others.

Today's Affirmation:

I will be faithful, loving and kind to others.

DAY 88: GENTLENESS

Mistreating someone because they mistreated us is unkind and rooted in pride and a desire for revenge. It is true that hurt people hurt people but retaliation is not the best way to deal with our challenges. Seeking revenge keeps us tied to events, robs us of our joy and peace and keeps us focused on the past rather than moving forward. When we're hurt, we have to swallow our pride and seek solutions and outcomes, not revenge, if we want to heal and move forward.

I used to be the queen of holding grudges, a habit I'm not proud of that I still grapple with occasionally. I made myself and those closest to me miserable when I decided to be prickly and holding onto anger when I could have resolved the conflict peacefully. I was controlled by pride, easily offended and I needed to "win" and be right. I thought being tough and holding grudges made me seem tougher when it actually weakened me. These habits cost me inner peace and peaceful relationships with others.

It's a beautiful thing to be broken and made whole through Him. Every place we're broken becomes a place where His light shines through and makes us whole again. We don't have to be tough or hardened to save face. Our capacity to be humble prompts God to exalt us. Humility doesn't make us weak, it keeps us strong. My favorite Joyce quote, "God knows the mess we're in when He calls us. His light shines greater through 'cracked pots' than it does through those who have it all together," is posted on my vision board and it rings true.

Each of us makes mistakes. The best thing we can do is humbly admit our errors, face them and do our best to help others when they make mistakes and forgive them when they've hurt us. It's not an easy thing to do but it's the best thing to do to preserve our inner peace and joy.

Today's Affirmation:

I will learn from my mistakes and use them to grow and help others.

DAY 89: SELF-CONTROL

Pietro Aretino once said, "I am, indeed, a king, because I know how to rule myself." This is a true and profound statement. Here's the tough part – it isn't always easy to control ourselves but it is vital. Our capacity to use self-control determines our ability to live in our purpose and fulfill our destiny.

Self-control helps us prevent impulsive behavior. Toddlers act impulsively because they haven't learned self-control. We know we shouldn't react or lash out in situations when it's best to be quiet or be still. Self-control requires us to act on what we know, not what we feel. Cool heads prevail in every situation. Controlling our impulses is an irreplaceable life skill.

I enjoyed watching the police procedural *The Shield*. Lt. Kavenaugh, a rogue member of the Internal Affairs Department, acted impulsively and recklessly in order to punish police officers he considered corrupt. He was so out of control while pursuing his targets, he became unhinged. Kavenaugh failed because he was unable to control his emotional impulses. He was ultimately terminated from the police department and served a prison sentence for the illegal things he did. His behavior and inability to control himself brought on his demise. Each of us displays Kavenaugh tendencies at times. Though he is a fictitious character, he's an excellent example of what happens when our emotions rule us.

Curbing our impulsive behaviors brings us one step closer to being more focused and successful. Instant gratification becomes less important and our goals seem more tangible. When we're focused, we can ignore the triggers that prevent us from thinking clearly and the distractions that keep us from accomplishing our goals. We cannot control those around us but we can control our response. Time is precious so choose carefully what you become involved in and who you become involved with. Allow less negativity and foolishness in your life and make room for more positivity and happiness.

Self-control is one of our greatest inner strengths. When we use self-control, it makes us champions because we become able to use our gifts at an optimal level. When we conquer self, we can conquer the world.

Today's Affirmation:

I will control my emotions. It's vital for me to use self-control to reach my destiny.

DAY 90: WE ARE ALL GIFTED

We've talked about nine special qualities over the past eighty-nine days and they are all qualities we need to cultivate and share to live quality, fulfilling lives. Love, joy, peace, patience, kindness, goodness, faithfulness, humility and self-control are connected rungs on a ladder to happier, more fulfilling lives.

Our world needs love more than anything else. So many people are hurting, lonely, stressed, overburdened and unhappy, yet the power of loving words and actions toward others is an easy way we can show **love** to others and add joy to their lives. It's easy to lose our **joy** if we concentrate solely on ourselves and the unhappy things we face each day but if we think more of the things that add to our happiness and look for ways to uplift other people, we can experience joy and scatter joy among others. When we feel and share love and joy, it adds to the **peace** and contentment we feel, making it easier for us to encourage others to feel in their lives.

Patience, the fourth rung on the ladder, can be challenging. We have to be patient with ourselves and others and life often shows us we need to develop our capacity to be calm and kind to others when they do or say something we don't like. Patience adds to our ability to show **kindness** to others through words and deeds. **Goodness** comes along when we treat others well whenever we have the opportunity to do so.

Faithfulness means we are reliable and loyal to what we say. It means we keep our promises. This is an irreplaceable quality in our relationships with others. **Humility**, an important quality in healthy relationships, is thinking of ourselves less than we do others. The final rung on the ladder, **self-control**, is vital because it means we have the ability to exercise restraint over our feelings, words and actions.

The good news is that each of us is capable of showing these nine qualities to others and ourselves. The reality is that it takes effort and commitment to do so. It won't always be easy but it is always worthwhile to climb this ladder each day. The experiences we have in our lives are lessons that remind us how important each rung of this ladder is. For example, when people mistreat us, we remember how important love, kindness and goodness are. When we lose our tempers, that's a lesson reminding us how important it is to use self-control and to remain at peace. When we're betrayed, we remember how important it is to be faithful and to show humility when others are hurt.

Michael Jackson's song *Man in the Mirror* is an ideal way to remember how important it is for us to do our parts to be more of what the world needs and to give of ourselves to make it possible. As Michael Jackson sang, "I'm starting with the man in the mirror, I'm asking him to change his ways, And no message could have been any clearer, If you want to make the world a better place, Take a look at yourself, and then make a change." That's why we have to look for shortcomings in others after we've looked in the mirror and fixed all of ours first.

Imagine what a wonderful world we could have if we looked more at what we can give and share instead of thinking about what we can receive. None of us are perfect but we are all capable of being our best. Please reflect on how you can be your best and how you can give your best to others.

Today's Affirmation:

I will show love, scatter joy, be at peace, be patient with others, show kindness and goodness, be faithful, show humility and practice self-control. It won't always be easy but I can do it if I don't give up.

THANKS

To my mother for being my first teacher, my motivator and for believing in my ability to communicate. Thanks for reminding me I have an important message to share.

To each of the special people who has remained with me through sadness, anxiety, the bleakest times and was patient enough to love and encourage me when I wasn't the most lovable, thanks for seeing the best in me. Thank you for staying when it would have been much easier to walk away.

To the man who inspires me to be my best, pushes me and supports me, thank you. I appreciate you and the special role you play in my life.

Thanks to Terry Boykin for designing the cover art exactly as I envisioned it!

To each person who read this book and finds a way to use the motivation and encouragement I've shared, thank you. I'm blessed you shared the final leg of the journey with me. Keep climbing the ladder of love, joy, peace, patience, kindness, goodness, faithfulness, gentleness and self-control and making your life and the lives of those around you happier.

Made in the USA
Middletown, DE
22 August 2017